THE
WAR YEARS

LIFE IN BRITAIN DURING
1939 TO 1945

THE
WAR YEARS

LIFE IN BRITAIN DURING
1939 TO 1945

JANICE ANDERSON

Futura

A Futura Book

First Published by Futura in 2007
Reprinted in 2009

Copyright © Omnipress 2007

ISBN: 978-0-7088-0743-9

Produced by Omnipress Ltd, Eastbourne

Printed and bound in Singapore

Futura
An imprint of
Little, Brown Book Group
100 Victoria Embankment
London EC4Y 0DY

Photo credits: Getty Images

An Hachette UK Company

CONTENTS

'PEACE FOR OUR TIME!'

Sunday, 3 September 1939, was a beautiful day in England – 'a fine, sunny morning, apples shining', noted Virginia Woolf in her garden in Sussex. Like many others the length and breadth of the country, she had just heard Great Britain's prime minister Neville Chamberlain announce on the BBC wireless that, because Germany had made no undertaking to halt its invasion of Poland, a country with whom Britain had treaty obligations, the country was once again at war with Germany.

Most people were not surprised. Horrified, hugely distressed and sickened perhaps, but not surprised. As the 1930s progressed, the threatening activities in Europe of Germany's Fascist chancellor Adolf Hitler in his pursuit of 'lebensraum' for Germany had made war look increasingly likely. And Italy's Fascist leader Benito Mussolini had also been flexing his muscles throughout the decade, invading Abyssinia (present-day Ethiopia) in 1936.

APPEASEMENT

'Appeasement' was the British government's answer to the actions of Germany for much of the 1930s. Exhausted and deeply in debt after the Great War of 1914–18 and battered again by the Depression of the early 1930s, Britain was in no state to fight another major war. Neville Chamberlain's last attempts at appeasement came during September 1938. After a flight to Munich to join the French prime minister Edouard Daladier in talks that the two leaders hoped would persuade Hitler not to invade Czechoslovakia and thus avert war, Chamberlain returned to England, waving a piece of paper in the air at Heston Airport and crying that he brought back 'peace with honour'. Later, he told a great crowd in Downing Street that he had brought 'peace for our time'. 'Our time' lasted less than a year.

AIR WARFARE

Britain had been bombed from zeppelins and twin-engined bombers during the 1914–18 war, and the government accepted that in any future conflict, air warfare would bring the country as much in the line of fire as its fighting forces overseas. In September 1939, Britain's people knew that they would soon be fighting on a 'home front' as dangerous and as full of death and destruction as any battle front.

THE KING BROADCASTS TO THE EMPIRE

'There may be dark days ahead, and war can no longer be confined to the battlefield. But we can only do the right as we see the right, and reverently commit our cause to God. If one and all we keep resolutely faithful to it ... then with God's help we will prevail. May he bless and keep us all.'

– George VI, addressing the nation via the BBC, 3 September 1939.

▲ *Peace In Our Time*
30 September 1938: British prime minister Neville Chamberlain (1869–1940) making his 'peace in our time' address at Heston Airport on his return from Munich.

▶ *War Broadcast*
4 September 1939: George VI (1895–1952), King of Great Britain (1936–1952), making his radio broadcast to the nation after the outbreak of World War II.

THE HOME FRONT

With its appeasement policy looking increasingly unlikely to succeed, the British government had begun preparing for the inevitable in the mid-1930s.

PROTECTING THE HOME FRONT

Defence spending and planning for an integrated home defence and anti-air-raid system were stepped up, as was spending on bomber command so that Britain would be able to take the war to the enemy. The devastating effect of bombing from the air, demonstrated not only by the Italians in Abyssinia but also by German and Italian fascist forces in the Spanish Civil War, concentrated minds on how best to deal with the great number of casualties and widespread devastation from the all-out strike on the British mainland that officials had long thought would be the inevitable start to any war with Germany.

AIR RAID WARDENS' SERVICE

An Air Raid Wardens' Service, set up in April 1937, was an integral part of Britain's Civil Defence organisation. In January 1938, the first Air Raid Precautions Act, based on the findings of a secret air-raid precautions subcommittee set up as far back as 1924, came into force. By September 1939, local authorities, empowered by the Act, had established a properly planned Air Raid Precautions (ARP) system involving ARP warden command posts (most of them very basic concrete boxes, surrounded by sand-bags), as well as other Civil Defence services, such as emergency ambulance services (which in London included taxis, comman-

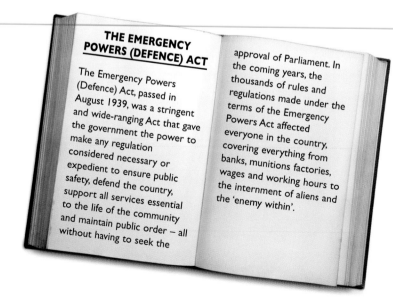

THE EMERGENCY POWERS (DEFENCE) ACT

The Emergency Powers (Defence) Act, passed in August 1939, was a stringent and wide-ranging Act that gave the government the power to make any regulation considered necessary or expedient to ensure public safety, defend the country, support all services essential to the life of the community and maintain public order – all without having to seek the approval of Parliament. In the coming years, the thousands of rules and regulations made under the terms of the Emergency Powers Act affected everyone in the country, covering everything from banks, munitions factories, wages and working hours to the internment of aliens and the 'enemy within'.

▲ *25 February 1939: Two women in Islington, London, try out the height of their new air raid shelter, distributed by the government as protection against German bombing raids.*

1939

JANUARY

4 President Roosevelt calls for an increase in the US defence budget.

5 Hitler demands the return of Danzig to Germany.

9 Hitler reopens the *Reichstag* building, which was destroyed by fire in 1933.

10 Chamberlain meets with Mussolini in Rome.

17 Germans pass a law forbidding Jews to drive cars.

19 The former president of the *Reichstag* is dismissed by Hitler after daring to issue a warning that Germany's rearmament programme threatened the economy.

24 Gestapo officer Reinhard Heydrich was asked to speed up the evacuation of the Jews from Germany.

30 Hitler threatens the Jewish race during his *Reichstag* speech.

FEBRUARY

10 Poland closes the Danzig Corridor to German road and rail traffic.

14 The German battleship *Bismarck* is launched.

19 Poland and the Soviet Union sign a trade agreement.

23 Jews are ordered to hand in any precious metals and stones.

deered for the work and painted grey), first aid posts, a rescue, repair and demolition service, and local fire services expanded by the creation of an Auxiliary Fire Service.

During the anxious days of August and September 1938, local authorities had begun digging trenches in public parks and gardens. However, these were not to be filled in, and weeks before war was declared digging was increased so that by 3 September 1939, an estimated 500,000 people could have sheltered in trenches, guided to them by 'To the

1939

MARCH

13 Berlin demands the dismissal of anti-Nazi ministers from the government.

15 Hitler marches into Prague, effectively bringing about the end of Czechoslovakia.

20 The USA recall their ambassador from Berlin as a protest to the German invasion of Czechoslovakia.

28 Spanish Civil War ends. Franco is in control of Madrid.

31 Britain and France join forces, declaring their intention to defend Poland against any aggressors.

APRIL

3 Germany makes plans to invade Poland.

7 Italy invades Albania.

20 Hitler celebrates his 50th birthday with a military parade in Berlin, and the day is declared a national holiday.

26 Compulsory military service is proposed by British government.

28 Hitler revokes a 10-year non-aggression pact with Poland.

Trenches' notices in city streets – a dreadful reminder for many older men of the trench warfare they had experienced on the Western Front in the Great War.

Barrage balloons, or 'blimps', first seen in the sky over London in August 1938, also appeared again, at first mainly over London, and air-raid sirens were sounded, so that people would recognise their meaning: 'enemy bombers approaching, take shelter'. And there were piles of sandbags everywhere, protecting doorways to important buildings, entrances to underground stations, first aid posts, shops and restaurants – and the statue of Eros in London's Piccadilly Circus. Few people, many believing either that diplomacy would avert a war that nobody, either British or German, wanted, or that if war came it would be quickly over, thought in 1939 that they would be living with barrage balloons, sandbags, air-raid sirens and officious ARP wardens for six long years.

It was that other great anti-air-raid innovation, the blackout, that helped make ARP wardens often unpopular with the general public, especially householders. Since it was essential that no chink of light should show to guide enemy night-time bombers to populated areas, blackout rules were stringent, both inside houses and out in the street, and many was the householder ordered by an officious ARP warden or policeman to turn out his lights. ARP wardens were all local men and women, familiar with the streets they patrolled and with such important details as who lived in what house, who lived alone and where fire hydrants, gas-main covers and electricity boxes were.

THE BLACKOUTS

At home, between the hours of sunset and sunrise, householders had to put up blackout material over all windows and other openings through which light might show. This meant that every night (beginning on 1 September 1939 at half an hour before sunset) Britain's homeowners had to spend some time going round their houses, pulling curtains so tightly that no chink of light showed and sealing doors, windows, fanlights and skylights with black fabric or paper, cardboard and thick paper. Since this could take some time in larger houses, many people left the black fabric or cardboard over non-essential windows, or

▲ *Pedestrians, including a mother and child, wearing gas masks as they pass a notice saying 'Warning. Tear Gas is Being Discharged'.*

even painted them with black paint. Blackout materials had to remain in place until half an hour after sunrise. Many also criss-crossed their windows with sticky tape, to prevent flying glass in the event of a bombing raid.

Not surprisingly, blackout fabrics, paint and cardboard soon disappeared from shops. Also not surprisingly, chinks of light did show, and householders were often disturbed by the sound of their front-door bell or knocker (painted with luminous paint so that it would show up in the dark) being operated by the firm fingers of an irate ARP warden or policeman, quick to point out deficiencies.

Many householders also thought it prudent to take measures against a gas attack. Poison gas had been a terrible scourge on the Western Front in the Great War, and officials had to assume that the Germans would use it again. When things were looking very black for the future of Europe in the summer of 1938, the government had issued gas masks – thirty-eight million of them – to every man, woman and child in Britain (babies had to wait until the first months of the war to get their own, very awkward-to-wear, gas masks). As well as issuing gas masks, the government also directed that gas contamination stations and Local Gas Identification Squads, recruited from among qualified chemists, must be set up. Street cleaners were trained to deal with its effects and people were alerted to the types of gas they might encounter, including tear gases, lung irritants and blister gases, and how they might smell. At home, householders tried to keep one room sufficiently sealed with cellulose sheets and tape to make it gas-proof.

Outside in the street, the blackout regulations were so stringent that they caused more deaths and accidents than the enemy – who did not actually cause any on mainland Britain in the first months of the war – and had to be slackened somewhat. The government's first blackout order was to turn off all street lighting, all shop lighting and all neon advertising signs. Citizens could not carry torches, or even light a cigarette. Whether or not to go out after dark became a major decision for many; one housewife considered the night she 'came through the blackout for the first time on my own' so momentous that she recorded it in her diary.

The total night-time blackness was supposed to be alleviated for pedestrians and motorists by the white lines that were painted on kerbs, walls, trees and lamp posts. That they were far from successful was demonstrated by the fact that in the first

month of the war, the number of people killed in road accidents nearly doubled. Then there were the many who were injured, often seriously, by tripping over unseen kerbs and sandbags, driving into walls and trees, stepping off railway station platforms, even walking into streams and canals.

Clearly, the country could not carry on having one citizen in every five injured in

▶ *Illuminated Helmets*
A Salford policeman prepares illuminated helmets for wear when assisting pedestrians and traffic during the blackout hours of winter.

▲ *Workmen prepare for emergency blackouts in London during World War II by providing alternative street lighting, 24 August 1939.*

DEALING WITH GAS MASKS

Gas masks were ugly, even grotesque objects. Adults' gas masks had an unattractive pig's snout shape and smelled of rubber and disinfectant; children's came in a Mickey Mouse shape, with red rubber face pieces and shiny eye-piece rims. As for babies, their strangely shaped masks were so designed that mothers had to pump air into them with a bellows. Naturally, everyone hoped that they would never have to wear theirs. As the threat of gas attacks receded – and there was no punishment for not carrying one's gas mask in its cardboard box – so they were either not carried at all or forgotten about and left behind in shops and cinemas, in the office, on buses and trains.

1939

MAY

12 German attacks on Polish property in Danzig.
22 Nazis sign a 'Pact of Steel' with Italy.
31 Germany and Denmark sign a 10-year non-aggression pact.

JUNE

7 Germany signs non-aggression pact with Latvia and Estonia. Start of deportation of Jews to Poland.
23 France and Turkey sign a mutual defence treaty.

JULY

9 Winston Churchill proposes a military alliance with Russia.
17 Poland decides to declare its opposition in case Germany attacks Danzig.
31 Polish customs officals are ordered to leave Danzig; Poland responds with economic sanctions.

AUGUST

20 Hitler announces that 'the destruction of Poland will start on Saturday morning' in a speech to his generals.
23 Hitler and Stalin sign a non-aggression pact.
24 Poland mobilises her forces ready for war.
25 Poland and Britain sign a Mutual Assistance Treaty.

1939

AUGUST

27 The world's first jet engine, the Heinkel He-178, makes its maiden flight.

29 Poland is given an ultimatum by Hitler on the subject of Danzig and the Polish corridor.

30 Civilian evacuations begin from London.

31 British fleet mobilises.

SEPTEMBER

1 Germany invades Poland. Italy, Norway, Finland, Switzerland and Ireland proclaim their neutrality.

3 Britain, France, Australia and New Zealand declare war on Germany.
German submarine *U-30* sinks British passenger ship *SS Athenia*, mistaking it for a warship.
German forces penetrate the Polish Corridor and Belgium declares its neutrality.

4 British Royal Air Force attacks the German Navy.

5 USA declares neutrality; German troops cross the Vistula River into Poland.

6 South Africa declares war on Germany.

8 German Army reaches the outskirts of Warsaw.

10 Canada declares war on Germany and the Battle of the Atlantic begins.

11 Upper Silesia now in German possession.

▲ *Evacuees from London in Guildford, Surrey.*

SAFE AND NOT-SO-SAFE BRITAIN

Evacuation scheme planners divided Britain into three areas. 'Evacuation areas' were danger zones – those parts of the country, such as London (the seat of government), urban areas, the great industrial cities and major military installations, thought to be most at risk of aerial bombardment and therefore the regions that people would be evacuated from. 'Reception areas' were those parts of the nation, mostly rural and western coastal areas, considered safe to receive evacuees. 'Neutral' areas neither sent people away nor received evacuees. Later events showed that the scheme, if fully implemented, would have had major flaws: the dockyard cities of Plymouth, Swansea and Bristol, left off the evacuation areas list because they were thought to be too far west to come within range of Hitler's Luftwaffe, were all heavily bombed.

▲ *Labelled evacuees waiting for their train out of London.*

some way because of the blackout regula-tions, and within a few weeks they were relaxed. People were allowed to carry a torch at night, provided its light was covered with a double layer of tissue paper and it was switched off during air-raid alerts – and pro-vided, too, that one could purchase both the torches themselves and the batteries to keep them working.

Other rulings that were relaxed within a few weeks of the war's beginning were those that had closed all theatres and cinemas and stopped football matches and other events at which large numbers of people might come together. This was because the government was sure that the war would start with a massive air strike on the British mainland and that the best way of preventing unmanageable

1939

SEPTEMBER

13 The German High Command announces civilian targets will be bombed in Poland.

14 Royal Navy sink a German submarine U-39 in the Atlantic.
Warsaw is surrounded and the majority of the Polish Army is destroyed.

16 Germans demand surrender of Warsaw.

17 Russia invades Poland.
German U-boat sinks British fleet carrier *Courageous*.

19 Hitler makes a triumphant entry into Danzig.
Russian and German troops merge, ending the Polish campaign.

20 First air battle between the RAF and the Luftwaffe over Germany.

25 Warsaw suffers major air attacks.

27 Warsaw surrenders following heavy bombardment.

29 Germany and Russia divide up Poland.

30 Polish government set up in exile in Paris.
Royal Navy begin an all-out search for the German battleship *Graf Spee*.

numbers of casualties was not to let people gather together in large numbers. When the expected air strike did not materialise, by which time it had been realised that keeping people marooned in their homes and away from social contact was extremely bad for morale, cinemas and theatres were opened again and the football programme swung into action.

EVACUATION

For families with young children, the prospect of war was dreadful indeed. The independent organisation, Mass Observation, which had been studying British society since 1937, found some mothers so fearful for their children that they said they would consider killing them in the event of war. Most people, more measured in their response, chose instead to think about sending their children away from likely danger areas. Many children were sent abroad, to North America and other countries of the Empire, especially Canada and Australia, but the great majority of children, if they were sent away at all, were sent to places within Britain, most of them by way of the government's mass evacuation scheme.

In deciding to keep their children in Britain, parents had before them the example of the king and queen. King George VI and Queen Elizabeth had two daughters, and there had been some talk about sending the princesses to Canada for the duration. Nothing came of this, Queen Elizabeth saying that their daughters would not go without her, she would never leave the king and the king would never leave his country. So the princesses Elizabeth and Margaret Rose went to Windsor Castle; their London home, Buckingham Palace, was bombed several times during the war.

EVACUATION BEGINS

The evacuation of children, their teachers, pregnant women and mothers with babies from those parts of the country thought to be most in danger of aerial attack turned out to be another government scheme to prevent mass casualties that proved much more worthwhile on paper than in reality. The government had considered evacuating children from at-risk areas in September 1938 and therefore had evacuation plans ready. Operation Pied Piper, as the great evacuation scheme was code-named, began on 1 September 1939, two days before war was declared.

While the evacuation scheme worked pretty efficiently in getting away everyone who wanted to go – and, because the evacuation scheme was not compulsory, the majority who did not want to move could not be forced to – there were big problems in the reception areas. Although local authorities had made careful lists of billetors, most of whom came forward voluntarily so that the authorities did not have use their legal powers of compulsion, there were many problems about allocating children to the available billets. Often, something of a cattle market atmosphere prevailed, with people choosing children who looked most attractive, or large boys who could work on farms, or taking only one or two from a family of several children.

Although some evacuee children had a great time, discovering the joys of life outside big cities and getting on well with their new 'families', many, faced with unfamiliar customs, foods, living conditions and not very welcoming people, found life strange, lonely and frightening. Many missed out on regular schooling, once the schools opened again. As for the young mothers and pregnant women, life in the country was just boring. By the end of the year, some sixty per cent of evacuees had returned to their urban homes.

Although there were to be more movements away from the cities and industrial areas when the Blitz began in September 1940 and again during the V-1 and V-2 bombings of 1944–45, the government never again organised a large mass evacuation.

An important task for the government intent on protecting the home front was dealing with 'the enemy within' – including Britons such as the members of Oswald

▲ *Cupboard Shelter*
A day nursery in the East End of London, where the children shelter in a linen cupboard during an air raid.

Mosley's British Union of Fascists and foreign nationals living in Britain, who might be thought to be a danger to the state, perhaps spying for their home countries. There had been a steady stream of refugees from Germany and from Austria, most of them Jews fleeing Nazi persecution, into Britain in the 1930s. Although many of them moved on to North America and elsewhere, there were estimated to be in

1939

OCTOBER

1 Polish Navy surrenders.

9 Hitler orders preparations to be made for a massive offensive against France, Holland and Belgium.

12 Deportation of Austrian and Czech Jews to Poland begins.

14 British battleship *Royal Oak* is sunk at Scapa Flow by German U-47.

17 Hitler begins his euthanasia on sick and disabled in Germany and declares that the area of the *Reich* is to be 'rid of Jews, Poles and other unwanted elements'.

30 A White Paper is published in Britain regarding the horrors of Nazi concentration camps.

Britain considerably more than the 58,000 men, women and children in September 1939 who had officially registered since January 1938.

At the outbreak of war, the authorities gathered up and detained only those few hundred 'aliens' thought to be a real threat to national security. All Germans and Austrians in Britain, of whom there were over 73,000, had to appear before special tribunals to have their exact status verified. Some 570, considered to be possible security risks, were put in category 'A' and interned. Another 6,780 were put into category B, which made them subject to some restrictions and kept under supervision. The rest, the great majority of them refugees from Nazi oppression, came into category

'C' and were allowed to carry on with their daily lives unsupervised.

Calls for a mass internment of aliens, voiced loudly by Winston Churchill among others, became strident after the Germans, their actions rumoured to have been helped by 'fifth columnists', invaded the Netherlands on 10 May 1940, the day on which Winston Churchill replaced Neville Chamberlain as prime minister in Britain. Before the end of the month, the Home Office ordered the internment of all category B men between the ages of 16 and 70 and category B women between the ages of 16 and 60 who were not infirm, pregnant or had seriously ill children. When Italy declared war on Britain and France on 10 June, the government quickly decided to follow the advice of Winston Churchill, and 'collared' and interned all Italian men aged between 17 and 70 who had been living in Britain less than twenty years.

By mid-July 1940, some 30,000 people were interned, most of them in hotels and boarding houses on the Isle of Man. Some were shipped overseas, in appallingly cramped conditions, to Canada and as far away as Australia. When the *Arandora Star*, full of internees, was torpedoed and sunk with great loss of life in the Atlantic in July, the outcry against this punitive internment policy became loud indeed. Without saying anything official, the government quietly dropped the policy and internees began to be gradually released. By the summer of 1941, only about 5000 people were still interned. Most internees went on to do as much as possible to help the war effort in Britain and overseas, many of them in the armed forces.

British citizens likely to be enemies of the state were dealt with under the terms of

▲ *Refugee Boys*
German refugee boys returning from the fields at Flint Hall Farm, Hambledon. The boys are part of a scheme to train boys to become farmers and then settle them around the Empire.

▲ *Jewish Refugees*
11 August 1939: A young girl plays her violin to a friend. She is one of 150 Jewish refugee children to arrive as part of the 'Kindertransport' at Liverpool Street station from Berlin.

Defence Regulation 18B, passed on 1 September 1939. Several hundred members of the British Union were imprisoned under this regulation, including Oswald Mosley himself and his wife Diana, a Conservative MP, Captain Maule Ramsey and an ex-chief of Naval Intelligence. The Mosleys were not released from Brixton prison until the end of 1943.

So the United Kingdom battened down the hatches and prepared for war.

FINDING A SAFE PLACE

By the end of September 1939 something like a quarter to a third of the population of Britain had moved away from 'vulnerable' areas. Among these estimated 1,200,000 people were workers as diverse as thousands of civil servants, moved with their records to hotels in spas and seaside resorts, the BBC's Variety department (moved to Bristol) and its main centre staff (to a large country house in Worcestershire), and Bank of England staff, who found themselves in a small village in Hampshire. Editorial and layout staff of Good Housekeeping put together the magazine's first wartime edition 'on trestle tables set in the window recesses of a beautiful old castle' in Wales. The Principality also provided a wartime home for the contents of London's National Gallery, and many of the world's most important paintings were stored in a disused quarry 'for the duration'.

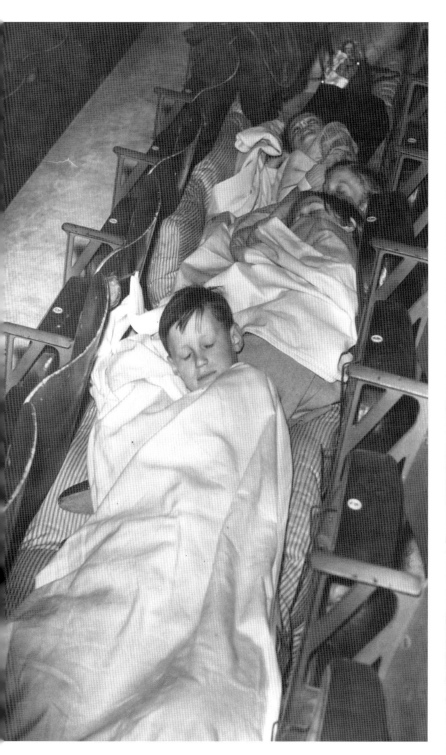

▲ *Seat Sleep*
Young Dutch and Belgian refugees sleeping in the seats at
Empress Stadium in Earl's Court, London.

1939

NOVEMBER

1 The Polish Corridor and Danzig now officially passed over to the German *Reich*, along with all the territories ceded to Poland under the terms of the Treaty of Versailles in 1919.

3 The neutrality bill put in place by the USA is amended to allow Britain and France to obtain arms.

8 Assassination attempt on Hitler fails.

23 Armed merchant ship HMS *Rawalpindi* sunk by German warships *Gneisenau* and *Scharnhorst* in the Atlantic.

29 Russia ends diplomatic relations with Finland.

30 Russia invades Finland.

DECEMBER

1 *Graf Spee* sinks British steamer *Doric Star* in the Atlantic.

13 *Graf Spee* is spotted off the River Plate estuary near Montevideo.

14 Russia is expelled from the League of Nations.

17 *Graf Spee* damaged in the Battle of the River Plate.

23 Various Latin American countries protest against the violation of their rights to neutrality by the warring nations.

25 Hitler makes a personal visit to inspect his troops on the Western Front.

FIGHTING THE WAR
ON THE HOME FRONT

Nothing much of a warlike nature happened in Britain in the first weeks and months of the war. At sea, the merchant navy came under attack at once, the liner Athenia *being torpedoed and sunk by a German U-boat (submarine) on 4 September with the loss of 112 civilian lives. It was not until November that the first bomb was dropped on Britain, in the Shetlands.*

It was an isolated incident, far from the massive all-out attack that everyone had expected. Even over in France, the British Expeditionary Force (BEF) was not seeing any serious action.

At home, many of the inconveniences and difficulties experienced by people came as a result of Britain's own, long-thought-out plans for the defence of the country being put into operation. All ARP systems were fully operational and the blackout had made Britain dark indeed between the hours of sunset and sunrise. Petrol rationing was introduced three weeks after the start of the war, and food rationing, announced to no one's surprise in November (there had been rationing during the Great War, after all), finally came into force in January 1940.

Conscription, which had been introduced for the first time in peacetime, by the Military Training Act of May 1939, when it applied only to young men of twenty and twenty-one, was extended to all men between eighteen and forty-one by the National Service (Armed Forces) Act, passed just two days before war was declared.

By this time well over a 250,000 men and women had already volunteered for the armed forces. Men in the uniforms of the Army, Royal Navy and Royal Air Force and women in their forces' uniforms – the Auxiliary Territorial Service (ATS), the Women's Royal Naval Service (WRNS) and the Women's Auxiliary Air Force (WAAF) – were becoming increasingly familiar sights in towns and cities the length and breadth of the country. And, as there had also been five times as many volunteers for the various Civil Defence services as for the armed forces, their identifying brassards (armbands) and uniforms, when they were given them, would soon also be just as familiar.

◄ *Aerial Cameras*
WAAF instrument repairers with aerial cameras on which they work. On left a F24, which can take 5 × 5 exposures either manually or automatically. The other two are G28 gun cameras, producing 2.5 × 2.5 inch negatives from a roll film.

1940
JANUARY

8 Rationing begins in Britain. Finland scores victory against Russia on the Karelian Front.

10 Belgium and Holland uncover plans of a German invasion.

13 Under threat of German invasion, Begium begins to mobilise its troops.

16 Hitler delays attacking West until the spring.

21 British destroyer *Exmouth* sunk by U-boat off coast of Scotland.

30 Hitler speaks out at the Berlin *Sportpalast*, and declares that the first phase of the war is complete with the destruction of Poland.

FEBRUARY

2 Big Russian offensive on the Karelian Front.

9 Fighting breaks out on the Mannerheim Line in Finland.

11 Russia and Germany sign an agreement regarding the supply of raw materials in exchange for military equipment.

15 U-boat war steps up a level on the orders of Hitler.

16 299 British prisoners freed from the German ship *Altmark*.

20 Russia and Finland begin new peace talks.

1940
MARCH

13 Finland signs a peace treaty with Russia.

16 Germany bombs Scapa Flow naval base near Scotland.

18 Hitler and Mussolini meet at Brennero. 'Il Duce' declares that Italy is now ready to join the war against Britain and France.

19 In reponse to the German attack on Scapa Flow, 50 RAF bombers raid the German base at Hornum on the island of Sylt.

▶ *Fire Training*
A team of firewomen belonging to the Royal Northern Hospital in Holloway, train their hose on an imaginary fire during practice for Blitz fires.

THE BORE WAR

People soon began to call this second great war of the twentieth century the 'Bore War', a play on words that recalled the Boer War at the end of Victoria's reign. That war had been fought thousands of miles away; perhaps this one would also be fought away from home. Gas masks began to be left at home (though their cardboard cases were often used as lunch boxes by schoolchildren), children were brought back from the 'reception areas' to their urban homes and families, and shops and restaurants began reducing the size of the barricades of sandbags, many of which were already rotting, they had built around themselves.

In March 1940, the 'bore war' – by now being called, American-style, the 'phoney war' – began to turn into something much more menacing for the home front. Four days after Finland, which had been fighting the Soviet Union's Red Army for four months, finally surrendered, a bomb, dropped by a German plane apparently mistaking a village for an airfield, or perhaps the Scapa Flow naval base, killed a civilian in the Orkneys. A German U-boat had already had one spectacular success at Scapa Flow. When the battleship *Royal Oak* was torpedoed in October 1939, 800 sailors had lost their lives.

At much the same time, the German war machine, having seen Eastern Europe carved up into German and Russian spheres of influence, turned its full attention westwards. It looked first towards Scandinavia. Here there were rich mineral resources as well as bases for German U-boats, already apparently winning the battle of the Atlantic, where British merchant naval losses had been considerable.

On 8 April 1940, the British and French followed up an anti-German navy mine-laying exercise they had carried out along the coast of Norway by sending a small expeditionary force to Narvik in an attempt to stop the transport of Swedish iron ore to Germany. The next day, Germany, ignoring Norway's declaration of neutrality, attacked the country with combined air, sea and land forces so effectively that within half a day they had seized several important Norwegian ports and towns, including Narvik and Trondheim. The fightback from Norway and Denmark, also attacked, was undermanned and under-resourced, and British support was not backed up by air cover. The result was inevitable. Denmark and Norway were occupied; British forces could not be withdrawn from southern Norway until June.

The greatest change at home resulting from the embarrassing Norwegian debacle was the replacement of Prime Minister Neville Chamberlain, by Winston Churchill, as prime minister and minister of defence in a Coalition Government, on 10 May 1940.

On the day that Winston Churchill became prime minister, Britain heard the dreadful news that the Netherlands, Luxembourg and Belgium had been invaded. France's Maginot Line, which the BEF was helping to defend, looked very vulnerable. The 'phoney war' was over. On 13 May, a Royal Navy destroyer brought Queen Wilhelmina of the Netherlands to Britain, and Churchill, in his first address as prime minister to the House of Commons, told the British people that he had nothing to offer them 'but blood, toil, tears and sweat'. Two days later, Holland surrendered and Germany's blitzkrieg ('lightning war') tore through Belgium (which surrendered on 27 May) and broke through the French defences into France. French and British forces retreated before them.

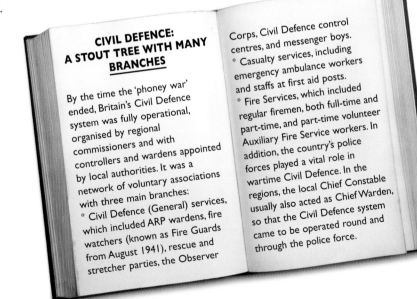

CIVIL DEFENCE: A STOUT TREE WITH MANY BRANCHES

By the time the 'phoney war' ended, Britain's Civil Defence system was fully operational, organised by regional commissioners and with controllers and wardens appointed by local authorities. It was a network of voluntary associations with three main branches:
- Civil Defence (General) services, which included ARP wardens, fire watchers (known as Fire Guards from August 1941), rescue and stretcher parties, the Observer Corps, Civil Defence control centres, and messenger boys.
- Casualty services, including emergency ambulance workers and staffs at first aid posts.
- Fire Services, which included regular firemen, both full-time and part-time, and part-time volunteer Auxiliary Fire Service workers. In addition, the country's police forces played a vital role in wartime Civil Defence. In the regions, the local Chief Constable usually also acted as Chief Warden, so that the Civil Defence system came to be operated round and through the police force.

▲ *Capture Of Narvik*
31 May 1940: The Norwegian town of Narvik burns after an Allied bombardment.

The first the British people knew that the BEF in France – an army with nine divisions, more than 250,000 fighting men and thousands of vehicles – was in desperate need of rescue from beaches in northern France, in a pocket around the port of Dunkirk (Dunkerque), was on 29 May. On that day a call went out for all sea-going vessels that could be brought into use to cross the Channel to help the Royal Navy in an evacuation operation, called Operation Dynamo, that had begun on 26 May.

An armada of 'little ships' – pleasure steamers, lifeboats, rowing boats, fishing smacks, coal barges, yachts and tugs – went across the Channel and helped the Royal Navy. By 3 June, nearly 340,000 men, including many French troops, had been evacuated from the beaches of Dunkirk. Left behind in France were the BEF's heavy weaponry, ammunition and equipment, either abandoned or destroyed, and more than 68,000 men killed, wounded or missing. Dunkirk was a retreat and a defeat, but

WINSTON CHURCHILL

Winston Leonard Spencer Churchill, who became Britain's wartime leader on 10 May 1940, was descended from the great eighteenth-century military commander John Churchill, 1st Duke of Marlborough. Born in 1874, Churchill entered parliament as a Conservative in 1900, but switched to the Liberal Party six years later. He played a busy and energetic political part in the Great War, first as First Lord of the Admiralty (a post to which he was returned on 3 September 1939), then as Minister of Munitions. An outspoken and often critical politician after 1918, Churchill, back in the Conservative fold in 1924, spent much of the 1930s in the political wilderness, almost the only voice warning against the threat of Nazi Germany. In May 1940, Churchill, by then 65, believed he had begun 'a walk with destiny' for which his whole life up to then had been a preparation.

1940
APRIL

9 Hitler invades Denmark and Norway in operation *Weserübung*.

10 First Battle of Narvik between the Royal Navy and *Kriegsmarine*.

13 Second Battle of Narvik, resulting in Royal Navy victory. Eight German destroyers sunk.

22 Inter-Allied Supreme War Council meet in Paris.

28 The Allied Supreme War Council of France and Britain decide neither will enter into a peace agreement with Germany.

▼ *New PM*
10 May 1940: Winston Churchill (1874 –1965) leaving a cabinet meeting at 10 Downing Street after his appointment as Prime Minister. With him are Air Minister Sir Kingsley Wood (1881–1945, left) and Foreign Secretary Anthony Eden (1897–1977, right).

▲ *Dunkirk Retreat*
Weary British soldiers waiting for
evacuation from Dunkirk.

Winston Churchill, while reminding the House of Commons that 'wars are not won by retreats', still managed to turn it into a powerful morale-booster for the nation. The 'Dunkirk' spirit' that Churchill invoked helped get Britain through the war.

The soldiers of the BEF, who returned to Britain to a heroes' welcome, with cheers, flag-waving and cups of tea, rather than the recriminations many of them had expected, found that they would not be alone in the defence of the nation. There was now a newly formed volunteer organisation, called 'Local Defence Volunteers' to help them.

On 14 May, people listening to the BBC's Home Service after that evening's nine o'clock news bulletin had heard Secretary of State for War, Anthony Eden, announcing that he was forming a new local defence organisation, which he called Local Defence Volunteers (LVD), that would give ordinary citizens, 'especially those not eligible to enrol in the armed forces', the chance to help in the defence of their country 'in its hour of peril'. He asked men who were British subjects and aged between seventeen and sixty-five to register at their local police station. They would not be paid, but they would be given uniforms (which they were – eventually), weapons (also eventually) and training.

THE HOME GUARD

The BBC's nine o'clock news bulletin the next night could have reported that some 250,000 men had already answered Eden's call – far more than the government had hoped or expected. By the end of June, the number of volunteers had reached one and a half million. From July, they were no longer called Local Defence Volunteers, Winston Churchill himself deciding that the name was uninspiring. Officially, the men were now members of the Home Guard; unofficially, because many of them were quite old and because in their first weeks they had no uniforms, no weapons (apart, perhaps, from a World War I rifle bayonet welded to a pole, or a pitchfork), and no training, they were soon dubbed 'Dad's Army'.

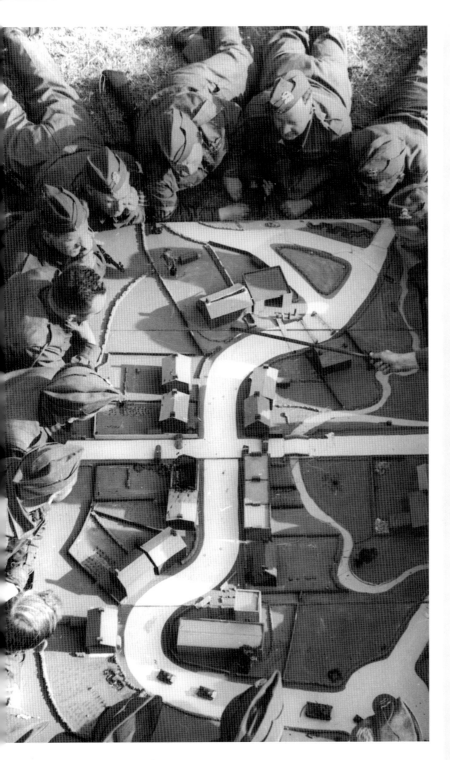

▲ *Home Guard Training*
*Home Guardsmen learn village defence at the War Office
Training School in Osterley Park, 21 September 1940.*

1940

MAY

1 Over 4,000 Norwegian troops surrender at Lillehammer.

10 Germany invades France, Belgium, Luxembourg and the Netherlands.
Winston Churchill becomes British prime minister.

13 German aerial raid on Rotterdam.
Britain begins recruitment for Local Defence Volunteers.

15 Holland surrenders to Germany.

17 RAF raid on Germany, hitting oil tanks in Bremen and Hamburg.

20 German troops reach the Channel coast.

26 Evacuation of Allied troops from Dunkirk begins.

28 Belgium surrenders to Germany.

31 68,000 Allied soldiers are taken off from Dunkirk.

JUNE

3 The Luftwaffe bomb Paris.
Dunkirk evacuation ends.

5 Battle of France begins.

7 British and French troops withdraw from Narvik in Norway.
French Air Force bomb Berlin.

9 Germany occupies Rouen and reaches the rivers Seine and Marne, making France virtually defeated.

10 Italy declares war on Britain and France.

The Home Guard, the largest civilian army ever formed in Britain, was, once trained and in uniform, a proficient and well-organised force, far from its 'Dad's Army' image. It knew all the basic army skills, from map-reading and reconnaissance to signalling in the field and carrying out night patrols, how to hunt, ambush and kill tanks, how to make Molotov cocktails, how to carry out street fighting . . . While it was never called on to carry out the more extreme of these tasks, the Home Guard was kept busy until mid-1944, manning anti-aircraft batteries and coastal defences, guarding arms and fuel dumps, and helping in Civil Defence work, including teaching men and women how to use guns. Their existence meant that the regular armed forces were freed to fight overseas while the Home Guard's help in the preparations for the D-Day landings of 1944 was vital.

France fell on 16 June 1940. 'I expect the Battle of Britain is about to begin,' Churchill told the House of Commons two days later. 'Let us therefore brace ourselves to our duties and so bear ourselves that, if the British Empire and its Commonwealth last for a thousand years, men will still say: "This was their finest hour."'

The Battle of Britain did not have clear-cut

THE MEN OF DAD'S ARMY

Many Home Guard men were too old for active service, others were either not yet old enough to join up or were in reserved occupations. In the beginning, motley gatherings of the local bank manager and MP, butchers, bakers and farm labourers, as well as ex-brigadiers, colonels and naval captains, might have looked unlikely defenders of the nation. In November 1941, membership of the Home Guard became compulsory, on a part-time basis, for all men aged between eighteen and fifty-four who were not in the armed forces or some other form of Civil Defence. At its peak, the Home Guard numbered over 1,793,000 men, 1,206 of whom died on duty.

▼ *Fighter Pilots*
July 1940: A group of fighter pilots from the 32nd Squadron at the RAF Fighter Squadron HQ at Hawkinge, Kent, relax on the grass. Left to right: R F Smythe; K R Gillman (killed in action 25 August 1940); J E Proctor; P M Brothers; D H Grice; P M Gardner; A F Eckford.

◄ *PO Home Guards*
21 June 1943: Members of the Post Office Home Guard receiving lessons on how to load the spigot mortar at a summer training camp in Hertfordshire.

start and finish dates. From about mid-June until mid-September, through a glorious English summer of fresh mornings and clear blue skies, Germany's air chief Hermann Goering launched his fighter planes against the RAF's bases. The destruction of the RAF and its airfields was essential to Hitler's invasion plan, Operation Sealion, which was timed to start on 15 September. Ironically, 15 September was the busiest day of the Battle of Britain, the Luftwaffe launching more than 1,700 sorties against southern England. After this date, the Germans, having failed to destroy Britain's airfields, changed tactics. Their invasion plan, postponed several times, was shelved. Britain's cities and industrial heartland would be bombed instead.

THE BLITZ

Now the Home Front really was in the front line. It would stay there for four long years, from the terrible Blitz of September 1940 to May 1941 to the V-1 flying bomb and V-2 long-range rocket attacks of 1944–45.

Hitler's attempt at an invasion of Britain did not come in the form of parachute troops landing out of the sky, as had happened in Europe and which Eden had anticipated in his BBC announcement of the formation of the Local Defence Volunteers in May.

◄ *Guess Who*
A young gunner in the London Home Guard demonstrates camouflage techniques. With his face and hands blackened, he uses old wallpaper to disguise himself at his post.

Instead, the air-raid sirens, last heard by many on the day that Neville Chamberlain told the British people they were at war, wailed over London again in the late afternoon of 7 September 1940. The Blitz, a long-drawn-out blitz-bombing of Britain from the air, had begun.

The sound of the sirens was within minutes succeeded by a heavy, droning hum as hundreds of enemy bombers approached. Then came the thuds of thousands of bombs exploding, many of them incendiary bombs to start fires, and most of them in the East End docklands. The All Clear sounded at 6 p.m. But the fires burning in the East End acted as a marker for the Luftwaffe, who came back two hours later. This time, the All Clear did not sound until 4.30 the next morning.

Up until 7 September, nearly 4,000 British civilians had already been killed or wounded by the enemy. The attacks that started on 7 September were of a very different intensity. The numbers of enemy aircraft involved were huge, and their raids on London went on for fifty-seven nights without a break. There were also many daylight attacks. Nor did the Luftwaffe confine its attacks to the East End and the City. Within a week, the West End was being targeted, too.

In the coming weeks, many familiar West End buildings, from the John Lewis Oxford Street department store, which was completely burnt out, to Buckingham Palace, hit twice within four days, were bombed. 'Now we can look the East End in the face,' remarked Queen Elizabeth, before putting on her best coat, her pearls, her most spritely hat and a pair of high heels to visit the people and the bomb sites of the East End. The king and queen and the prime minister all grasped early on their importance as morale-boosters.

In the front line of the defence of local neighbourhoods during the Blitz was the ARP warden. The warden, usually a part-time volunteer, with one in six of them a woman, often worked for two and even three nights in a row. The normal ARP warden count was six to a post, with one post for every five hundred people. It was the ARP warden's job to report each bomb fall to the local control centre, which in turn allocated

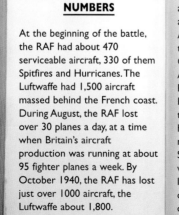

BATTLE OF BRITAIN NUMBERS

At the beginning of the battle, the RAF had about 470 serviceable aircraft, 330 of them Spitfires and Hurricanes. The Luftwaffe had 1,500 aircraft massed behind the French coast. During August, the RAF lost over 30 planes a day, at a time when Britain's aircraft production was running at about 95 fighter planes a week. By October 1940, the RAF has lost just over 1000 aircraft, the Luftwaffe about 1,800.

In July 1940, the RAF had about 1,100 pilots, many just a year or two out of school. As well as British-born pilots, there were New Zealanders, Canadians, Americans, South Africans, Belgians, French, Poles and Czechs – and an Israeli and a Jamaican. A total of 307 of these men had been killed or listed as missing or captured by September. There were 300 wounded men. In all, Britain lost 537 airmen in the Battle of Britain, and Germany over 2,500.

1940

JUNE

11 Germany takes Rheims and the French government leaves Paris for Tours.

12 British surrender at St Valéry.

14 Germans enter Paris.

15 Germans open Auschwitz concentration camp.

16 Marshal Pétain becomes French prime minister.

17 German bombs sink troopship *Lancastria*.

18 Hitler and Mussolini meet in Munich.
Russians begin occupation of the Baltic States.

22 France signs an armistice with Germany.

23 Hitler tours Paris.

24 France signs a formal surrender with Italy.

25 All hostilites cease on French soil.

28 British government recognise de Gaulle as the 'Free French' leader.
German aircraft bomb the islands of Jersey and Guernsey.

30 German occupation of the Channel Islands begins.

JULY

1 Marshal Pétain establishes French government at Vichy.
German U-boats attack merchant ships in the Atlantic.

5 French government breaks off relations with Britain.

the emergency services (fire, ambulance and heavy rescue). When the emergency services arrived, the warden had to be on hand to direct them to fire hydrants, gas mains and those damaged buildings that were most likely to have people still inside.

Also of huge importance during the Blitz were volunteer fire watchers (later turned into an official arm of Civil Defence called the Fire Guard). Armed with just a bucket of sand and a stirrup pump, the men and women who acted as fire watchers for the long months of the Blitz saved many a building. They put incendiary bombs out of action by dumping sand on them, while the fine spray from a stirrup pump dealt with firebombs more safely than the heavy douse of water from a hose, which could cause bombs to fragment. It was fire watchers on the roof of St Paul's Cathedral, drawn from the cathedral's own staff, who saved Wren's masterpiece from destruction, allowing its dome to rise defiantly and triumphantly above the smoke and flames of the burning city.

On the last really heavy bombing day of the Blitz in London, 10 May 1941, the Mansion House and fourteen hospitals were hit, 2,000 fires raged across London, and the chamber of the House of Commons was destroyed. Winston Churchill made sure he was photographed for the newspapers and magazines, his familiar hat, overcoat and walking stick all in place, standing indomitably amidst the ruins of the House of Commons.

German bombers soon extended the range of their attacks beyond London, attacking major ports from Liverpool to Plymouth, the Midlands' industrial heartland and transport and communication links between Britain's big cities. Two of the most devastating raids outside London took place in Birmingham and Coventry, already the targets of dozens of attacks, in November. In Coventry on 14–15 November, nearly five hundred and seventy people were killed, the city's great medieval cathedral was destroyed and many factories were severely damaged; within days, most of the factories were patched up and working again. It was much the same in Birmingham, where a raid lasting eleven hours on 22–23 November started nearly 600 fires and killed almost 800 people.

▲ *Damage In City*
Damaged buildings in Cannon Street in the City of London during the Blitz.

1940

JULY

10 First phase of the Battle of Britain begins with German air attacks on Channel convoys.

13 The first Free Polish Fighter Squadron of the RAF is formed.

19 Hitler speaks at *Reichstag* and urges Britain to see reason.
Denmark withdraws from the League of Nations.

20 Destroyer *Brazen* sunk by German aircraft.

23 Russia takes Lithuania, Latvia and Estonia.
British government introduces a severe new form of taxation in the third 'War Budget'.

28 All rail and road links are cut between France and Vichy by the Germans.

29 Dover Harbour attacked by German bombers.

AUGUST

2 The Vichy Government sentence de Gaulle to death during his absence.

3 Italy occupies British Somaliland in East Africa.

5 Hitler and Mussolini meet in Rome to discuss strategies after the defeat of France.

8 Heavy air battles over the Channel, with Britain claiming 80 German losses in one week.

10 HMS *Transylvania* sunk by U-56 off coast of Ireland.

TAKING SHELTER

From now on, the British people, exhorted by Public Information posters and leaflets to 'KEEP CALM and CARRY ON' stifled their terrors as best they could and did just that. People got on with their daily lives, sheltering at home from night-time bombing raids under the kitchen table, in the cupboard under the stairs, in the cellar, in the Morrison shelter in the living room or the Anderson shelter in the garden. Caught outside, people took shelter where they could, often under bridges or railway arches, in road tunnels and even in natural shelters such as caves; by October 1940, the Chislehurst Caves in Kent were sheltering 15,000 local residents.

There were supposed to be in all towns and cities good numbers of public shelters, suitable for people to stay in during bombing raids which, it was wrongly assumed by planners, would be short and intense. Such shelters might be in civic building basements or office buildings, in which space was requisitioned for the purpose, or they might be purpose-built. The latter were mostly brick boxes with concrete roofs, too small, without the facilities necessary to shelter large crowds for long periods, and liable to collapse if a bomb went off near them. There were never enough of these deeply unpopular public shelters, partly because of arguments between government and local authorities over who should pay for them.

Londoners had the Underground. At the start of the war, the Home Secretary, fearful of allowing large numbers of people to gather together and wanting to keep the Underground fully operational, refused to allow its stations to be used as shelters. Londoners had other ideas, and poured down into the Tube when the sirens wailed in September 1940. At first conditions below ground were pretty squalid, but gradually improved as better lighting and sanitary facilities were installed, canteens and some 22,000 bunk beds were made available and regular cleaning was carried out. Some stations even laid on entertainment; in others, people made their own, with sing-songs being the order of the night in many. (Some

▲ *Neighbourhood Shelter*
Mrs Sant of Mytton Street, Manchester, watch men recruited from a Mutual Aid Committee
construct a dug-out in the grounds of her home to be used for shelter during air raid attacks.

people took earplugs below ground with them, along with books, knitting and other essentials, in order to get some sleep.)

IN THE CHANNEL ISLANDS

While the people of mainland Britain were enduring the Blitz, the people of the Channel Islands were having to come to terms with German occupation. The British Government had decided, albeit reluctantly, that in the

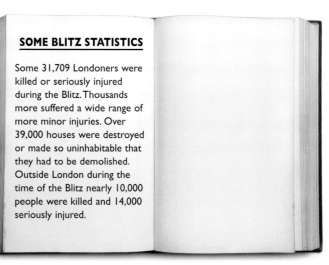

SOME BLITZ STATISTICS

Some 31,709 Londoners were killed or seriously injured during the Blitz. Thousands more suffered a wide range of more minor injuries. Over 39,000 houses were destroyed or made so uninhabitable that they had to be demolished. Outside London during the time of the Blitz nearly 10,000 people were killed and 14,000 seriously injured.

event of war there was nothing they could do to protect these strategically unimportant islands, which had been British territory since the Norman Conquest. When war came, some 30,000 Channel Islanders were evacuated, leaving about 60,000 to sit out the war, hopefully too far from its main theatre to be of interest to the Germans.

But the Germans were interested, and on 28 June 1940, they bombed the two main islands, Jersey and Guernsey, killing forty-four people. Occupying forces began arriving on 30 June and by 3 July they had taken all four Channel Islands. They were the only part of British soil to be occupied by the Nazis during World War II. Their harsh treatment, which included internment, rigorous ordering of all civilian social life, severe reprisals for any acts of disobedience or resistance and, after a year or two, little fuel, no electricity and considerable hunger, was a good indication of how the mainland would have suffered if Hitler's Operation Sealion, planned to start on 15 September 1940, had not been thwarted by the RAF and the Battle of Britain.

▲ *Christmas Underground*
20 December 1940: ARP members hang Christmas decorations in a cubicle of a shelter beneath a cinema in South London.

IN THE UNDERGROUND

At the height of the Blitz in London, around 177,000 people were spending their nights in a Tube station, regulars being given bed tickets. Those without bunks slept on the escalators, along the platforms and even in hammocks slung over the rails – once the power had been cut off for the night. Sheltering in the Underground did not guarantee safety. Sixty-four people died when Balham Station was bombed in October 1940, and 111 at Bank Station in January 1941.

▲ *Rocket Damage*
Rescue workers at the scene of a V-2 rocket attack on
Farringdon Market in London during World War II. One, a
nurse, has the letters CS on her tin helmet.

1940

AUGUST

11 Battle of Britain begins in earnest as 400 German planes attack the coasts of Britain.
12 Luftwaffe attacks Portsmouth, Isle of Wight and the Kent and Sussex coasts.
13 German bombing offensive against airfields and factories in Britain.
17 Hitler announces total blockade of the British Isles.
23 First German air raids on Central London.
25 First British air raid on Berlin.
31 RAF Fighter Command lose 38 planes in Luftwaffe attacks on their HQ.

OCTOBER

4 Hitler and Mussolini meet in an armoured train at the Brenner Pass to discuss war progress.
9 Winston Churchill is voted as leader of the Conservative Party.
18 Britain reopens the Burma Road.
27 General de Gaulle forms the Free French Government in opposition to the Vichy.
28 Italy invades Greece.
31 British civilian casualties for the month of October amount to 6,334 killed and 8,695 injured.

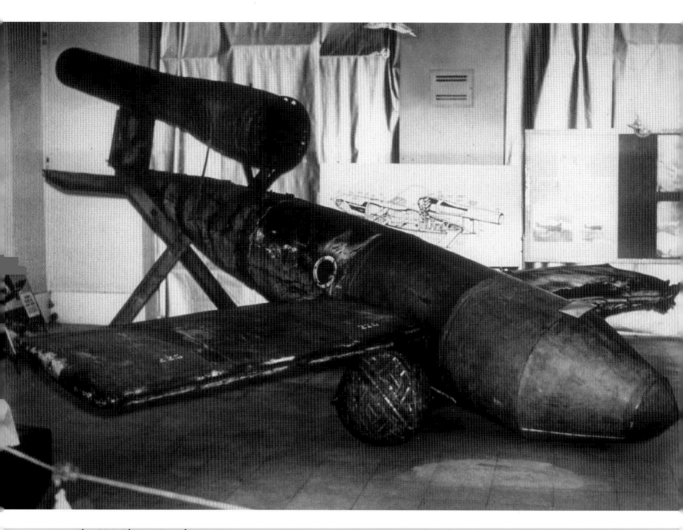

▲ *V-1 Flying Bomb*
circa 1944: A German V-1 Flying Bomb.

▶ *Blitz Cricket*
A group of men playing cricket on a blitzed site during their lunch hour, with St Paul's Cathedral in the background.

THE DOODLEBUG

The worst of the war on the mainland seemed to everyone to be over by June 1944. The Allies had already landed in Europe, having sent over to Normandy on 6 June 1944 the largest seaborne invasion force the world had ever seen. Then came the V-1 and V-2 attacks, which were of a very different order from the bombings of 1940–41.

To start with, they were unexpected. And the weapons had been developed in great secrecy.

Hitler believed that his new secret weapons would change the course of the war; they came too late for that, but they did cause considerable damage, both in terms of the destruction and death they wrought and in terms of the morale-depleting dread they caused.

The V-1 (short for Vergeltunsgwaffe Eins, or Retaliation Weapon One), was a jet-propelled unmanned aircraft carrying an explosive warhead. Launched from sites in

Germany, 2,450 of them came over London and south-east England in the second half of June 1944. Their approach was heralded by a puttering whining sound that got them the names 'buzz-bomb' or 'doodlebug'. Far worse than the puttering sound was the silence that succeeded it when the engine cut out. This meant that the V-1 was coming to earth, to explode on whatever, or whoever, was under it. As the blast effect of the V-1 was much greater than that of conventional bombs, so the devastation it caused was much more horrific and widespread. By September 1944, over a million Londoners had been evacuated from the city; many more left of their own accord.

By early September the V-1 attacks had petered out. Then came the V-2s. Between 8 September 1944 and 27 March 1945, when the last one landed on Orpington in Kent, some 1,050 V-2s fell on England. They were rockets, moving too fast to be intercepted – or even heard – and came down almost vertically. The first anyone knew they were there was the sound of an enormous explosion. Fortunately, Germany's use of the V-2, the world's first true ballistic missile, was halted when advancing Allied forces knocked out their launch bases in France.

At last the Home Guard could be stood down. As 1945 progressed, Britain could begin seriously to believe that victory – and peace – would soon come.

THE ARMED SERVICES
AT HOME

Britain's military manpower was far from being at full strength in September 1939. During the 1930s, the government had concentrated its military spending on home protection and on deterrence, building up the country's defensive air shield and bomber command at the expense of the Army, in terms of both manpower and equipment.

At the same time, Neville Chamberlain, after he became prime minister in 1937, had said that he would not consider bringing in conscription in peacetime.

Events during the signing of the 1938 Munich Agreement had given a boost to recruitment, not only to the ARP services but also to the military services, especially the Territorial Army and the RAF Volunteer Reserve. However, the government, remembering the rush to volunteer in 1914, which had badly depleted manpower in several essential industries, tried to check this spate of volunteering by publishing a Schedule of Reserved Occupations in November 1938.

With war soon looking more and more likely, it was clear that manpower in the armed forces, especially the Army, was well below strength and must be increased. Chamberlain changed his mind about conscription and, in April 1939, in the teeth of stiff opposition in the Commons and out in the country from the Labour Party and the trade union movement, the government drove a conscription bill through Parliament.

Conscription did not give a man any choice about which of the services he went into, and the Military Training Act, combined with the scare Munich had given the nation, gave a boost to voluntary recruitment. This is because, in theory, volunteers could choose which service they wished to enter. In fact, because the Army was most in need of recruits, the majority of volunteers were directed into it anyway.

By December 1939, more than one-and-a-half million men were experiencing the rigours of military training and discipline, which meant, if they were in the Army, about three months of basic training in barracks. More than two-thirds of them were in the Army, with the remainder being almost equally divided between the Royal Navy and the RAF. In addition to the men, 143,000 women, all of them volunteers, were serving in the women's auxiliary services – the Auxiliary Territorial Service (ATS), the Women's Royal Naval Service (WRNS), where they were called 'Wrens', and the Women's Auxiliary Air Force (WAAF) – and in various nursing services attached to the armed forces.

▶ *ARP Poster*
28 September 1938: A British government recruitment poster for the ARP (Air Raid Precautions) issued during the 'Phoney war' period before World War II.

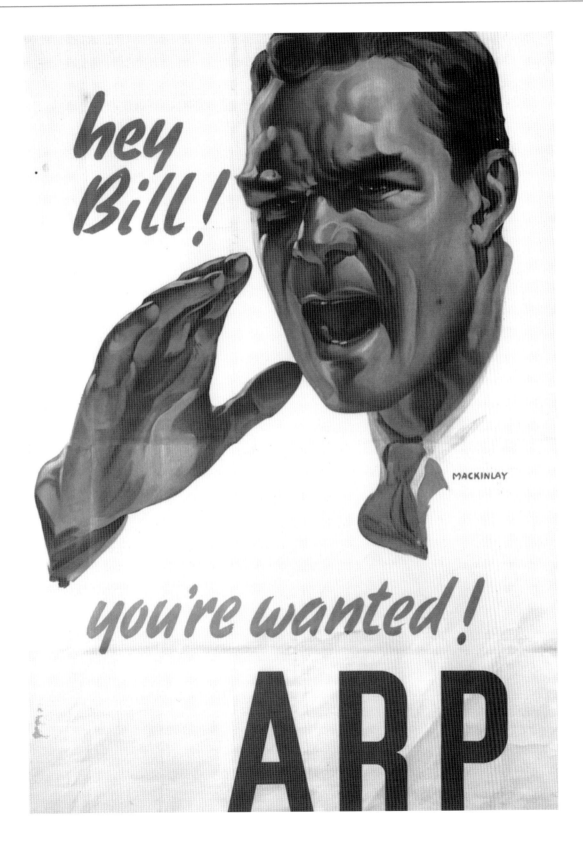

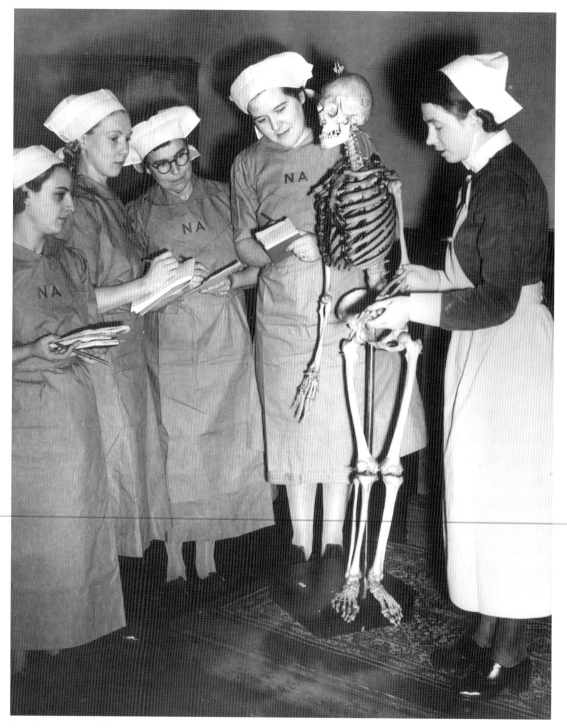

▲ *Nursing Auxiliaries . . .*
Nursing Auxiliaries receiving instruction on anatomy at the Booth Hall Hospital, Manchester.
Nursing Auxiliaries supplement hospital staff and man first aid posts as well as carrying on
with their civil jobs as far as possible.

For most of the war, about one-and-a-half million British service men and women were stationed at home, working in home defence, anti-aircraft, logistical training and administrative units. After Dunkirk, there were few theatres of war abroad that British troops were well enough equipped to be sent to, and the armed services concentrated on re-grouping and re-equipping in preparation for the time when they could move on to the attack, if not in Europe then certainly in the Middle East and North Africa, where British and Dominion forces began enjoying some notable successes in 1941.

As well as the British forces, there was, among the servicemen sent from the countries of the Empire and Commonwealth, a large contingent of Canadians, which had arrived in Scotland in December 1939. They had been intended for fighting in Norway and in France, alongside the BEF, but events prevented either deployment. For two long years the Canadians helped in the defence of Britain and saw no action in Europe until the disastrous Dieppe Raid of August 1942. They next saw action in the Mediterranean in 1943 before joining Montgomery's 8th Army in Italy.

COMPULSORY MILITARY SERVICE

Conscription was brought into Britain for the first time in peacetime by the Military Training Act, signed into law in May 1939. The Act made all men liable for call-up when they reached their twentieth year. If accepted, they would be trained and would serve full-time for six months, then would serve part-time for three-and-a-half years in Territorial units. The day war was declared, the conscription age was widened to cover men aged between eighteen and forty-one. In December 1941, the upper age limit was extended to fifty-one.

1940
NOVEMBER

1 Turkey declares its neutrality in the Graeco–Italian war.

3 First British troops arrive in Greece.

5 President Roosevelt is elected president of the USA for a third term.
Armed merchant cruiser *Jervis Bay* is sunk by battleship *Admiral Scheer* in the Atlantic.

10 A torpedo bomber raid cripples the Italian fleet at Taranto, Italy.

12 Soviet foreign minister Vyacheslav Molotov arrives in Berlin for talks with Hitler.

14 Germans bomb the city of Coventry.
Greek troops push Italians back into Albania.

19 Birmingham is bombarded by Luftwaffe bombs for over nine hours.

20 Hungary agrees to join the Axis powers.

22 Greeks defeat the Italian 9th Army.

23 Romania joins the Axis alliance.

24 Slovakia joins the Tripartite Pact.

26 The Jewish ghetto in Warsaw is sealed off from the rest of the city.

31 British civilian casualties for November amount to 4,588 killed and 6,202 injured.

1940
DECEMBER

1 The Greek Army continue to push back the Italians.
2 Luftwaffe carry out night raids on Bristol.
5 Hitler lays out plans to invade Russia.
7 RAF carry out night raid on Düsseldorf.
8 Italy asks Germany to intervene in the war with Greece.
9 Operation Compass. British begin a western desert offensive in North Africa against the Italians.
12 Over 20,000 Italians are taken prisoner during Operation Compass.

▶ *ARP Exercises*
Wardens rescuing one of the 'casualties' during ARP exercises in Westminster.

APPLYING FOR 'CO' STATUS

For those men who, for reasons of moral, religious or political conscience, felt they could not fight, life became difficult when conscription was brought in. The National Service (Armed Forces) Act, which had widened the ages at which men were liable for conscription, had also set up a Military Services Register, on which were put the names of all men liable for military service. A man objecting to his name's being put on the Register could apply to be put on a Register of Conscientious Objectors instead. He would have to argue his case before a local tribunal.

At the start of the war, some twenty-two out of every thousand men from the first age group liable for service applied to be

▲ *Canadian Soldiers*
  circa 1940: A Canadian soldier gives the thumbs-up sign as he arrives in Britain.

▲   *Bomber Pilots*
World War II British airforce bomber crew walking in front of aircraft. From left to right:
Observer, Wireless Operator, Rear Gunner, Second Pilot, Pilot Captain.

registered as conscientious objectors. A minority of these Conscientious Objectors (or COs, as they came to be called) were given unconditional exemption from call-up; others were exempted on condition that they registered for other, non-military work, usually in Civil Defence or on the land; many requests for exemption were rejected entirely. Exemptions were granted in widely varying numbers from local authority to local authority. It could have become something of a post-code lottery but for the fact that conscientious objection dwindled as the war progressed; by mid-1940, only about six men in every thousand were applying for CO status.

THE RAF AND WAAF

When the war turned from 'phoney' to the real thing and the main battle zone was in the skies over southern England, especially during the Battle of Britain and the Blitz that followed it, the most hard-worked of Britain's military services were the RAF and the WAAF. The RAF provided the fighter pilots in the air and the technical crews on the ground. The WAAF provided many members of the staff in the operations rooms, where incoming enemy planes were tracked, their courses plotted and intercept directions were sent to the pilots in the air.

The RAF was greatly helped by being able to use the still top-secret radar. A chain of what looked like radio masts but which were, in fact, radar stations, had been built along the coast to give advance warning of incoming Luftwaffe planes. Radar meant that the RAF did not have to waste manpower and fuel keeping patrols in the air, but could get them airborne from their bases in time to met the incoming bombers and their fighter escorts. The huge value of radar was demonstrated when the Luftwaffe knocked out the radar station at Ventnor on the Isle of Wight, punching a large hole in the protective shield offered by radar that took ten days to fill.

The whole pattern of the armed forces' presence in Britain changed dramatically

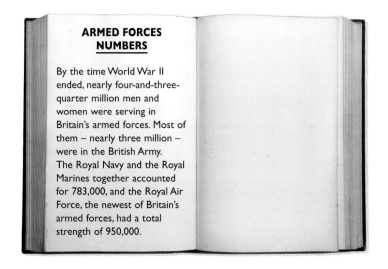

ARMED FORCES NUMBERS

By the time World War II ended, nearly four-and-three-quarter million men and women were serving in Britain's armed forces. Most of them – nearly three million – were in the British Army. The Royal Navy and the Royal Marines together accounted for 783,000, and the Royal Air Force, the newest of Britain's armed forces, had a total strength of 950,000.

1940
DECEMBER

13 German troops move into Romania from Hungary.

17 British troops rech Sollum near the Libya border and the Italian situation becomes critical.

22 Aircraft from HMS *Illustrious* bomb Tripoli.

26 After a brief Christmas respite, the Luftwaffe resume their bombing of London.

29/ Massive German air raid
30 on London

31 British casualties for the month of November are 3,793 killed and 5,244 injured.

after the Japanese bombing of Pearl Harbor in December 1941 brought the United States of America into the war on the Allied side. Hitherto, the Americans had hoped to keep out of the war, which was seen as a European thing, and their help for Britain after the fall of France had been in the very practical form of the Lend-Lease programme, which brought Britain much needed replacement armour and ships.

United States forces began arriving in Britain in January 1942. By 1943, American GIs were 'over here' in such large numbers that they formed by far the largest single block of non-British servicemen in the country. The GIs were in Britain to help develop the great invasion plan that went into action in June 1944. American airmen were here to strengthen the air attack on Germany. With the arrival of the Americans, the war against Germany went on to the offensive.

GETTING TO KNOW YOU

American servicemen were issued with leaflets introducing the very different culture they were about to encounter. They learned that language differences lay in more than pronunciation; American suspenders were British braces, pants were trousers, faucets were taps, erasers were rubbers (a tricky one, since an American GI's rubber was a Briton's condom). They also had to come to terms with warm beer, a lack of central heating, pretty inadequate bathrooms and driving on the left-hand side of the road.

British men soon realised that the average American – 'overpaid, over-fed, over-sexed – and over here', as comedian Tommy Trinder put it – was very attractive to British women, who liked the Americans' relaxed approach to life, and the chocolates, cosmetics and silk stockings they could get from their canteens. Black GIs came as a shock to the British, not just because most of them had never encountered black people, but also because of the 'colour bar' in operation in the US forces.

▲ *American soldier and his English girlfriend*
This couple are chatting about places to see and things to do while relaxing on the lawn in London's Hyde Park, a favorite haunt for lonely GIs.

WARTIME WORK

'Getting on with the job' took on a whole new meaning on the home front during the war. For those who stayed in their pre-war jobs, working conditions, for bank manager and milkman, shopkeeper and bus driver alike, became increasingly difficult.

People got used to walking to work past damaged buildings and across rubble and broken glass, perhaps after a night spent fire-watching or on ARP duty, or sleeping in an Anderson shelter or down in the Underground.

Once at their place of work, they might sweep up the glass and stick a notice saying 'More open than usual' on the door, or dust down their desks and write letters that might have to be delivered by hand by a member of staff assigned to the job or by teams of special Post Office workers. For other workers, jobs and working conditions changed radically. Factories switched from their peace-time manufacturing to war production, making silk parachutes instead of Viyella shirts perhaps, or wooden aeroplanes, such as the wood-fuselage Mosquito fighter-bomber instead of wooden furniture.

Many factories kept working seven days a week, their labour forces working 10–12 hour shifts. Wages were controlled and strikes banned. Tea breaks, at first limited because they interrupted production, were quickly recognised as being essential for workers' morale and health. From quite early in the war it became compulsory for factories to set up workers' canteens (in many of which the availability of cigarettes became as important a matter as getting a cup of tea). By the end of 1944, there were some 30,500 workers' canteens in factories in all parts of Britain.

War put an extraordinary strain on Britain's workforce, which soon found itself in a tug of war between the requirements of the armed services and those of the industries that supplied them while also supplying the nation. In the early months of 1940, when unemployment was high in Britain, the government did not think that there would be a problem about finding men to volunteer for all the new jobs that a wartime economy created, despite the increased demand for

1941
JANUARY

2 In retaliation for their defeat in Libya, the Italians launch a counter-offensive in Albania with the help of the Luftwaffe.

5 Italians surrender at Bardia, North Africa.

10 HMS *Illustrious* is hit by Axis aircraft while in a convoy on its way to Malta.

11 German aircraft hit HMS *Southampton* in the Sicilian channel and one Italian destroyer sunk.

19 British advance into Eritrea from Sudan.

21 Tobruk in North Africa is attacked by British and Australian forces.
Destroyer *Hyperion* is sunk by a mine off Cape Bon, Tunisia.

29 British advance into Italian Somaliland from Kenya.
Anglo-American talks begin on the consequences of US entry into the war.

◄ *Delivery After Raid*
A milkman delivering milk in a London street devastated during a German bombing raid. Firemen are dampening down the ruins behind him.

fighting men. Ernest Bevin, the energetic minister of labour, was sure that following a policy of 'voluntaryism' would get the men needed to do the jobs.

The government had also considerably depleted the potential armed forces recruitment pool in the British workforce with its Reserved Occupations scheme of January 1939. Under the scheme, some five million men over a certain age, which differed from one occupation to another, in a wide range of occupations, from boiler-making, skilled engineering and lighthouse keeping to doctors and teachers, were exempted from military service.

While the government had made one step towards controlling the movement of labour in June 1940 by bringing in a Dockers Registration Order, under which dock workers had to register so that they could be moved to wherever in the country they were most needed, it was still seriously under-estimating the effect of the Army's man-power requirements on industry. In August 1940, at the height of the Battle of Britain,

the Army said that it would need 357,000 recruits by March 1941, followed by another 100,000 a month thereafter. A leading civil servant, Sir William Beveridge was appointed to head a new Manpower Requirements Committee, the purpose of which was to create a detailed numerical and statistical survey of Britain's manpower requirements so that future demand could be assessed and fulfilled.

Beveridge's report, available in December 1940, shook the government severely. In essence, the report said that there were not nearly enough workers in Britain to supply the Army with the numbers of recruits it was demanding while leaving enough men working in the munitions industry to produce the amount of arms and armaments this greatly expanded military force would need.

During 1941, largely as a result of the Manpower Requirements Committee's report, Britain's workforce was radically reorganised by the Ministry of Labour, Ernest Bevin having accepted that 'voluntaryism' would have to be replaced by compulsion.

WINNING THE BATTLE OF BRITAIN IN THE FACTORIES

Fighter aircraft production, unable to produce aircraft fast enough to replace those lost in operations over Europe, was turned into a Battle of Britain-winning operation by the Canadian-born newspaper magnate Lord Beaverbrook, who was made minister of aircraft production by Churchill in May 1940. Following his personal motto – 'Work without Stopping' – he drove the workers on Britain's aircraft production assembly lines through a punishing (and ultimately unsustainable) regime from early June to early November 1940 that produced an average of 62 Hurricanes and 33 Spitfires every week. Where Britain's aircraft industry produced some 4,280 fighter planes in 1940, Germany's managed less than half that number.

▲ *Shipbuilding*
Two ship builders at work, their work vital for the continuation of waging war against the enemy.

◀ *Milk Break*
1941: A factory worker drinking his daily quota of milk, in between grinding bomb shells. In factories where the atmosphere contained a high percentage of lead, workers drank a quantity twice a day to counteract the quality of the air they breathed.

1941
FEBRUARY

5 British armoured column intercepts Italian retreat south of Benghazi, Libya.

6 Australians capture Benghazi.

7 Battle of Beda Fomm on the north coast of Cyrenaica.

11 British forces advance into Italian Somaliland in East Africa.
The Luftwaffe sink five British merchant ships off the Azores.

12 German General Erwin Rommel arrives in Tripoli, North Africa.

14 First units of German 'Afrika Korps' arrive in North Africa.

The Reserved Occupations scheme was revised so that distinctions could be made within the reserved occupations between those firms doing essential war work and those whose output was inessential to the war effort. In the former, the ages at which workers could be reserved was lowered, while scheduled ages were revised upwards in the latter. By the end of 1941, there were some 100,000 firms on the Ministry of Labour's Protected Establishments Register.

Bevin also brought in a scheme, by way of a Registration of Employment Order published in March 1941, that allowed the government to direct people to essential work. The scheme began with the registration of men aged over forty-five and – with great reluctance, for the government did not like the idea of ordering women into work – women of twenty and twenty-one (extended upwards to thirty by the end of the year).

Also made law in March 1941 was an Essential Work Order. This covered some four-and-a-half million workers in those privately owned factories in engineering, aircraft production, shipbuilding and building industries as well as the railways and mining, that the Ministry of Labour had decided were doing work of national importance in wartime. Unless they conducted themselves very badly indeed in the workplace, these workers could not be sacked nor could they take leave from work without the permission of the local National Service Office.

Well aware of the importance of having good relations with the workforce and their trade unions in wartime, Bevin and the

HELPING 'UNCLE JOE'

An extra burden was put on British manufacturing output in 1941 when the Soviet Union was invaded by its former ally, Germany. The Russians, far from buckling under the German onslaught, stood firm. Now one of Britain's allies, Russia had to be helped. Lord Beaverbrook orchestrated a 'Tanks for Russia' week in September, during which every tank that came off the assembly lines, often produced in factories working double time, would be shipped to Russia and the Eastern Front. The first tank for Russia off the assembly line was named 'Stalin'; others had slogans like 'One for Joe' chalked on them. Most of the tanks, and aircraft, raw materials and food supplies, a lot of which was paid for by an Aid to Russia fund set up by Mrs Clementine Churchill, were sent to Russia's ice-free port of Murmansk in merchant navy Arctic Convoys.

Ministry of Labour tried to design labour policies that would avoid confrontation as much as possible while also doing something to increase job security and improve working conditions. Even so, and despite strikes having been declared illegal in 1940, over a million working days were lost because of strikes and other industrial action, often backed by the trade unions, in 1941.

It was the sheer, grinding hard work for very long hours, often in pursuit of impossible-to-reach production targets, and often in factories just patched up after the latest bombing raid, that caused many of the strikes. On the whole, the authorities were careful not to go the full length the law allowed them by imprisoning striking workers. Overall, working life in Britain changing radically – and forever – during World War II. Compulsion, while it allowed the government to move workers to where they were most needed, also meant that people experienced a new mobility. Class and cultural differences became unimportant as people from different backgrounds and different parts of the country worked together, not just to defeat the evil of Nazism, but also to 'build a better Britain'.

▲ *Mine Boys*
Boys from a mining village who are helping to increase Britain's coal output during the war, on their first trip underground.

BEVIN BOYS

Labour shortages were serious in coal mining, an essential war industry. By 1943, the workforce was an ageing one with few volunteers coming forward. Ernest Bevin's 'Bevin Boys Scheme' of 1943 was another exercise in compulsion. Under the scheme, the names of all men of twenty-five years and under who had not yet enlisted were entered in a lottery from which ten per cent were selected by ballot to go down the mines. The scheme was very unpopular, and forty per cent of those selected objected. Very few objections were upheld and 147 men were eventually sent to prison for refusing to obey their direction to the mines. The Scheme could only be a short-term one, but it brought 21,800 young 'Bevin Boys' to join the 16,000 'optants' (men who had opted for coal mining when they were called up) into the mines and solved a wartime manpower crisis.

▲ *Tank For Russia*
19 September 1941: British women working on a tank destined for Russia, with 'Greetings to our Allies' chalked on the side in Russian.

THE CHANGING ROLE OF WOMEN

The major contribution of women to the war effort during World War I, which did more than the activities of the suffragettes to gain them the vote in general elections in 1918 (for those over thirty; twenty-one-year-olds had to wait until 1928), also speeded up the process of making women more acceptable to men in the workplace.

This process was hugely accelerated during World War II. Whether at home, at work, in Civil Defence, or in the armed forces, women played a big part in helping Britain win the war.

WOMEN AT WAR

At the beginning of the war, women could choose for themselves what their contribution to the war effort would be. At home, the women of the household found the necessary blackout materials and bought the tape that criss-crossed their windows even before war was declared. While it might be the menfolk of the family who erected in the garden the corrugated metal Anderson shelter, it was the women who made sure that it, or the understairs cupboard or the cellar, if their house had one, was stocked with emergency rations, blankets and torches or candles. It was also women who had the greatest say in whether or not to evacuate their children and sometimes themselves, from the danger zones.

As the war progressed and more and more men were called up, even from reserved occupations, many women got jobs in what had hitherto been pretty much male preserves, such as the railways, bus driving and captaining the transport barges that moved many essential materials along canals and waterways. Some of them moved into the air, ferrying aircraft, from fighters and bombers to transport planes, from the factories where they had been built or repaired to airfields and RAF stations. They overcame early male prejudice to man anti-aircraft ('ack ack') posts and to maintain and hoist the unwieldy barrage balloons, filled with 20,000 cubic feet (570 cubic metres) of hydrogen, that so effectively deterred low-flying enemy aircraft. Thousands more, while carrying on with their day jobs, also volunteered for one of the Civil Defence organisations, working as ARP wardens, auxiliary policemen, ambulance drivers, first-aid workers, fire watchers or in the Women's Auxiliary Fire Service.

▶ *Anderson Allotment*
A Clapham, south London resident watering the vegetables she has planted on the roof of her Anderson shelter built in the garden.

▲ *First 'Dustwoman'*
A female dustman carries a tub full of old cans back to her dustcart. Women in Ilford have become the first to work as dustwomen during the war.

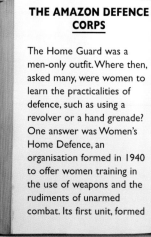

THE AMAZON DEFENCE CORPS

The Home Guard was a men-only outfit. Where then, asked many, were women to learn the practicalities of defence, such as using a revolver or a hand grenade? One answer was Women's Home Defence, an organisation formed in 1940 to offer women training in the use of weapons and the rudiments of unarmed combat. Its first unit, formed in June 1940, called itself the Amazon Defence Corps; by the end of 1942, there were said to be 250 Women's Home Defence units in the country. Technically, because they wore uniforms and provided weapons training (often given by Home Guard members), the units were private armies and therefore illegal. The War Office chose to turn a blind eye to their activities.

One of the most valuable contributions to the war effort a housewife could make was to join or help the Women's Voluntary Service (WVS). The WVS, founded in 1938 by Stella, Marchioness of Reading, was an almost entirely voluntary service. Of the hundreds of thousands of women – their exact numbers were never officially counted – who worked in its name during the war, only about 200 key workers were ever given more money than what covered their out-of-pocket expenses.

As the war went on, the women of the WVS, familiar figures in their uniform green-grey tweed suits, beetroot-red jumpers and felt hats, found work for themselves everywhere. Among the exhausted fighting men brought home from Dunkirk, it was the WVS who provide essential foot-washing facilities, washed and darned socks and served thousands of meals and cups of tea. During the Blitz, they kept up local censuses for the ARP services, organised convoys to get people out of heavily bombed neigh-bourhoods, drove canteens to the centre of clearing-up operations after a bombing raid, provided food and clothing for those who had been bombed out of their homes, and helped with the evacuation and care of children orphaned or separated from their families.

For women who preferred to work in the country, or who had liked gardening in peace time, the recruiting posters for the Women's Land Army, formed to provide essential agricultural workers to replace male farm workers now in the forces, sounded enticing. Women quickly joined the Women's Land Army in their thousands (80,000 of them by the end of the war), leaving behind jobs in shops and restaurants, offices and hairdressers to work on the land and grow and harvest the foods that the nation would need. Life was back-breakingly hard for most Land Girls, with the usual fifty-hour week extending to twice that long in harvest time, and with wages low, billeting arrangements often spartan and holidays few and far between.

Another out-of-doors wartime job that attracted some women was the Forestry Service. Here, women workers found themselves called 'Lumber Jills' or – perhaps less of a compliment – 'Polecats'.

1941
MARCH

1 Bulgaria joins Axis powers.
2 Germany occupies Bulgaria.
7 British forces arrive in Greece.
11 President Roosevelt signs the Lend-Lease Arms Bill which officially becomes law in the USA.
20 Four ministers from Yugoslavia resign rather than accept German terms.
24 British Somaliland is cleared of Italians, but Rommel reoccupies El Agheila.
25 Yugoslavia signs the Tripartite Act.
27 A coup in Yugoslavia overthrows the pro-Axis government and King Peter takes control.
Second phase of Battle of Keren in Eritrea ends in British victory.
28 Battle of Cape Matapan. Italy loses cruisers *Fiume*, *Pola* and *Zara*, while British only lose two aircraft.
30 Axis make counter-offensive moves in Cyrenaica, North Africa, with the help of the German 5th Light Division under Rommel.
31 British cruisers HMS *York* and *Bonaventure* are sunk by the Italians in a period of five days.

1941

APRIL

3 Pro-Axis regime set up in Iraq.
Germany marches into Hungary.

6 Germany invades Greece and Yugoslavia.
Allied forces enter Adis Ababa.

7 British promise allegiance to Yugoslavia.

8 British take Massawa in Eritrea.

9 Germans enter Thessaloniki and Rommel takes Bardia.

10 Germans enter Zagreb.
Hungary invades Yugoslavia.
Croatia made an independent state.

12 Belgrade surrenders.

13 Russia and Japan sign five-year neutrality agreement.

14 Rommel attacks Tobruk.

17 Yugoslavia surrenders to the Germans, RAF fly out King Peter.

19 Germany attacks Greece.
Empire troops land in Iraq.

20 British withdraw further into Greece and King George II heads new Greek government.

21 British troops asked to withdraw from Greece.

27 Greece surrenders to the Germans.
Axis forces cross Egyptian frontier as progress eastwards.

For many women with jobs when war was declared, it was a matter of just carrying on with them. Although World War I had shown that women could step into many skilled jobs in industry that had always been done by men, in 1939 the government was slow to consider suggesting that women should volunteer for work in factories and on heavy industry sites, both to replace men and to work alongside them.

It was not until January 1941, that the Ministry of Labour, abandoning 'voluntaryism', began directing workers to the industries where they were most needed. For the first time, Britain's women, instead of being asked to volunteer for work, were directed to jobs. At the beginning of the year, only women of twenty and twenty-one were directed to put their names on registers of employment; by the end of 1941 registration of women had been extended up to those aged thirty. In fact, the majority of women accepted suggested jobs, and few had compulsory directions issued against them. In May 1943, part-time work (which could mean up to thirty hours a week) became compulsory for all women aged between eighteen and forty-five. In all, some ten million women were registered for work, either full-time or part-time, by early 1943.

Perhaps the most momentous date in the whole war for Britain's women was December 1941, the month when the government announced, after months of deliberation, that women would be conscripted into some form of 'national service'. Britain thus became the first country in modern times to conscript women. The form that the conscription of women would take was clearly set out in the National Service (No. 2) Act, which became law on 18 December 1941. Only unmarried women, aged between twenty and thirty, would be called up. (Nineteen-year-olds were called up in the following year.) The women could choose between serving in the auxiliary services or in industry.

There was no great outcry against the conscription of women. Indeed, women – and the nation as a whole – had long foreseen that voluntary appeals to women were not working and that the country was desperately in need of workers and armed forces personnel, of both sexes. This was particularly so in the women's services. Many young

▲ *Salvage Depot*
25 November 1941: The WVS (Women's Voluntary Service) unloading salvage at a depot,
where it is to be sorted.

women had enthusiastically volunteered for the ATS, the WRNS and the WAAF in 1939, and were soon being seen out and about in their smart uniforms. But a great many of them had since thought better of it and had drifted away.

In April 1941, the government had attempted to halt the loss of female service personnel by making the women's auxiliary services officially part of the Armed Forces of the Crown. From July 1941, women enjoyed full military status – but were also now subject to

▲ *Baling Hay*
July 1942: Women of the Women's Land Army using a baling machine to bale hay on a farm in West Suffolk.

CLOTHES FOR THE BOMBED-OUT

The WVS was the nation's major provider of clothing for people who lost everything except what they stood up in during the Blitz. It had a nation-wide system of stores and depots, from which it distributed much-needed clothing, many tonnes of it sent to Britain from donors in North America and the countries of the Commonwealth. In the second half of 1940, the WVS distributed £1,500,000-worth of clothing.

▼ *Photographing WAAF*
A group of WAAFs prepare to have their photographs taken, after the announcement that the RAF was looking for the smartest WAAF to pose for a recruiting poster.

full military discipline. The National Service (No. 2) Act did not force women to undertake 'combatant duties' if they chose to join one of the women's services.

While most women in the armed forces found themselves in clerical or culinary jobs, there were jobs, such as those that took members of the WAAF into jobs at RAF stations, that put them very much in the front line. There were many interesting jobs available for women in the services, of course. Princess Elizabeth, the king's elder daughter, opted for service in the ATS when she was old enough. As well as learning to drive 'almost any kind of vehicle', as the recruiting posters put it, she, like many other women in the services, became adept at stripping truck engines and maintaining army vehicles.

By 1943, ninety per cent of single women in Britain and eighty per cent of married women were doing war work of some kind. Many of the seven million women in full-time civilian work were putting in long hours in engineering and munitions factories, turning out the machines and weapons that, within a year, would be helping in the great work of defeating the Axis powers. At the same time, the services were benefiting from the work of one-and-half million women now serving in Britain's armed forces.

▲ *Changing a Wheel*
A member of the Mechanised Transport Training Corps changes a wheel at an ARP post in Lambeth, south London.

▲ *Munitions Factory*
circa 1943: Women munition workers finishing shell cases during World War II.

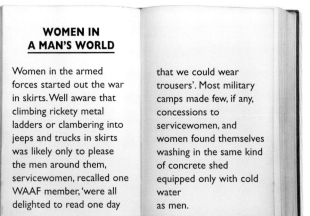

**WOMEN IN
A MAN'S WORLD**

Women in the armed forces started out the war in skirts. Well aware that climbing rickety metal ladders or clambering into jeeps and trucks in skirts was likely only to please the men around them, servicewomen, recalled one WAAF member, 'were all delighted to read one day that we could wear trousers'. Most military camps made few, if any, concessions to servicewomen, and women found themselves washing in the same kind of concrete shed equipped only with cold water as men.

1941
MAY

1 German attack on Tobruk is repulsed.

2 Iraqis attack British in Habbaniya.

5 Emperor Haile Selassie returns to his throne in triumph.

6 British triumphant over defeat of Iraqi forces.

10 Deputy Führer Rudolph Hess flies into Scotland.
Massive air raid on London – Westminster Abbey, House of Commons, Tower and Mint all hit. Record 1,436 people killed.

11 British bomb Hamburg.

15 Operation Brevity begins, which is the British counter-attack in Egypt.

16 Final British reinforcements arrive in Crete.
RAF night raids on Cologne.

18 New German warships *Bismarck* and *Prinz Eugen* sail into Baltic Sea.

19 Germans sink the Egyptian liner *Zamzam*, which was reported carrying 200 Americans, in the South Atlantic.
British occupy Fallujah in Iraq and bomb Baghdad airport.
Italian forces surrender to British at Amba Alagi in Ethiopia.

20 Germans commence invasionn of Crete in Operation Merkur.

THE WARTIME HOME

Everyone accepted that the family home was going to be in the front line in the war that started in September 1939. This meant that it would also have to be a bomb shelter, a refuge from gas warfare and a safe and strong store for food and water.

The householder got plenty of safety and protection advice from the government, in the form of an avalanche of pamphlets, leaflets and public notices delivered to every house in the land. However, the onus of putting that advice into practice fell firmly on the householder himself.

An early piece of home-protection advice offered householders by the government was a booklet, The Protection of Your Home Against Air Raids, published by the Home Office (price one penny) in 1938. This gave detailed advice on how householders could protect their property from the worst effects of bombs, incendiary devices and gas.

Gas was considered likely to be the most serious thing people would have to protect themselves from – hence the issuing of millions of gas masks, also in 1938. In the house, the Home Office booklet advised, people should create a 'refuge room', in which the fireplace, its flue stuffed with newspaper, should be boarded up with plywood and every crevice and crack in the room filled with putty or soggy newspapers. By the time the war actually started, few people remembered the booklet and fewer – if any – actually created a 'refuge room' in their homes, being much more concerned with ensuring that their blackout arrangements were perfect. By this time, too, the government was thinking along rather more practical lines when it came to protecting families.

The first shelter for family use, provided by the government before the outbreak of war, was the Anderson Shelter, named after the Minister of Home Security Sir John Anderson. Poorer inhabitants in recognised danger areas got their Anderson shelters free of charge; everyone else paid from £6 14s (£6.70) to £10 18s (£10.90) for them, depending on size. The standard-size Anderson shelter, intended for four people, or six at a pinch, was considered ideal for the average suburban family.

◀ *Gas Protection*
Three air raid wardens wearing a new type of gas mask, designed for the elderly and those with chest complaints, during a mock gas attack in which tear gas was released in Esher High Street.

1941
MAY

22/ Heavy German air attacks
23 on Crete sink cruisers *Fiji* and *Gloucester* and destroyer *Greyhound*. Luftwaffe sinks two more British destroyers *Kashmir* and *Kelly*.
24 *Bismarck* sinks the British ship *Hood*.
Hevy German bombing of Crete and King of Greece leaves for Cairo.
25 *Bismarck* escapes Royal Navy pursuit.
27 British Navy sink the *Bismarck* 400 miles (640 km) west of Brest.
Germans take Canea in Crete and British withdraw from the island.
Rommel recaptures Halfaya Pass on the Egyptian border.
28 Allied forces evacuate from Heraklion in Crete.
Roosevelt says that the Neutrality Act needs to be repealed.
29 Over 200 men killed when the destroyer *Orion* is attacked off Crete – two destroyers are lost.
30 A revolt in Iraq collapses as British approach Baghdad. Rebel leader Rashid Ali flees.

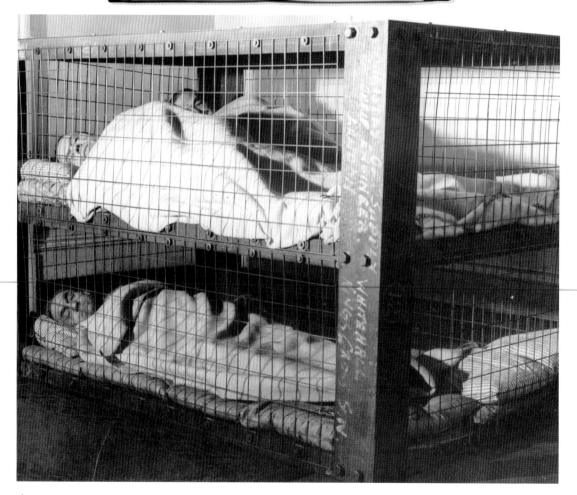

KEEPING WARM IN THE ANDERSON SHELTER

As the usual methods of household heating could not be used in the Anderson shelter, many ingenious forms of providing warmth were thought up. Drinks could be kept hot in Thermos flasks or in 'hay bottles', which were woollen bags packed with newspaper or straw. Two blankets sewn together made good sleeping bags, and a hot brick, heated in front of the fire for two hours, could be wrapped in something woollen and taken into the shelter to warm a bed. A warming heater could be made from two terracotta flowerpots: you simply fixed a candle at the bottom of one flowerpot (being careful not to block the drain hole) and put the second pot upside down on top of the first one. After a while, the 'heater' would give off noticeable warmth.

▲ *Two-Tier Morrison*
A group of men in the new two-tier Morrison shelter, similar in construction to the original indoor shelter, but housing two beds, one above the other. Where available, the new shelter will be supplied free to householders whose income is not more than £350 a year.

▲   *After The Air Raid*
The Dallison family leave their Anderson shelter to view the wreckage caused by a nearby bomb explosion the night before.

The Anderson shelter was a 'sectional steel shelter' intended for erection in the back garden (which meant it was most used in the suburbs, many inner-town houses having no garden), 6 to 15 feet (1.8 to 4.5 metres) from the house. The shelter was delivered in sections made of corrugated iron and had to be erected inside a hole at least 3 feet (1 metre) deep. The earth from the hole was put on top of the finished shelter to give added protection (and often, later in the war, to make a useful vegetable plot). Digging the hole and erecting the shelter was the householder's responsibility. Because they were partially underground, Anderson shelters were, at best, damp, draughty and cramped. Since they could quickly fill with water when it rained, the fire services spent much of their time in the early months of the war pumping out Anderson shelters.

Eventually, once people had got the hang of making their Anderson shelter more damp-proof (with the help of more leaflets from the government, including a Ministry of Home Security booklet called Air Raids – What You Must KNOW, What You Must DO, first published in 1940, then largely rewritten based on Blitz experience in 1941), the shelters, although not strong enough to withstand a direct hit, did give families good protection from near misses and flying fragments.

▼ *Clearing Up*
1941: Maintenance workers clear rubble in the City of London after an air raid.

Also surprisingly effective as a shelter, this time for indoors, was the Morrison shelter, named after the Minister of Home Security, Herbert Morrison, which was issued at the end of 1940. The Morrison shelter was a low, steel cage 6 feet 6 inches (2 metres) × 4 feet (1 metre 22 centimetres) in area and 2 feet 9 inches (82 centimetres) high, and with a sheet metal top. With enough room in it for a double bed-size mattress, the Morrison shelter could give a couple and their children shelter strong enough to withstand the weight of roof beams and other house debris falling on them.

As with the Anderson shelter, the Morrison shelter was available free to people with an annual income of less than £350, and at a cost of £7 to everyone else. Setting a good example, the prime minister was one of the first to have a Morrison shelter installed in his house, No. 10 Downing Street.

While something could be done to protect people in their homes, there was nothing that could be done to protect the houses. Although building was a reserved occupation, priority was given to the building of

▲ *Carry On Cooking 7 September 1940: Mrs WIlliams carries on with her cooking despite the fact her kitchen has no windows after a bombing raid.*

THE ENEMY'S HOUSING HIT LIST

A large part of the country's urban housing stock was destroyed by enemy action during the Blitz. The count for properties destroyed reached 3,250,000, with 92 per cent of the total reckoned to be private dwellings. Some figures for outside London: Sheffield, December 1940, 6,000 people left homeless; Merseyside, 'May Week' 1941, 70,000 people left homeless; Glasgow, Clydeside after raids in March, April and May 1941, only eight out of 12,000 houses left undamaged; Plymouth, March/April 1941, 'scarcely a house seemed habitable' to a Mass Observation team sent to the dockyard city; Portsmouth, May 1941, 60,000 of the city's 70,000 housing stock damaged to a greater or lesser degree.

▲ *Ruined Home*
*A man with a few belongings he has managed to salvage from his home, which was reduced to
a pile of rubble during a 'flying bomb' air raid.*

factories, accommodation for servicemen and women and other government contracts. Housebuilding virtually stopped when the war started and many men who had worked in the building industry of the 1930s, as civil engineers or builders, were, once the initial great increase in government building had ended, sent into the armed forces. At the same time, the government had placed strict controls on the use of building materials. Then came the Blitz. Long before it had ended, it was obvious that replacing destroyed homes and repairing those that

were damaged was going to put an enormous demand on men and materials.

With the Blitz at its height, the government began releasing men from the army to work in the Directorate of Emergency Work's special mobile squads, which were sent into local authority areas where they were most needed. In April 1941 a 16,000-strong squad of builders and repairers was sent into London, where some 39,000 houses were either destroyed or had to be demolished. By August, the squad had helped repair 1,100,000 houses, making them at least wind-and-weather-proof and therefore habitable. Another 50,000 houses awaited their attention.

This sort of first aid for housing was all very well in the short term, but it did not provide the country with social housing of either the quality or the quantity that was needed. The housing situation was aggravated by the constant population movements – evacuees to safe areas, workers to new factories thrown up on the outskirts of once quiet towns and villages, and billeted soldiers and civil servants. Then, when much housing repair and rebuilding had taken place, came the V-1 and V-2 attacks of 1944–45 to destroy much more property in the south-east than the Blitz bombings had achieved. The housing situation remained dire in many parts of the country throughout the war.

The great wartime increase in the numbers of marriages in Britain also added to the demand for housing – and on furniture to go in them. Young married couples naturally would like to start their new homes with new furniture, but the government was certainly not going to provide the materials, especially the wood, needed to make it. The price of second-hand furniture rocketed, and there was much profiteering in the furniture-making industry, so much so that the government was forced to step in and establish pricing rules and regulations.

By late 1941, officials were talking of Utility furniture, as they had recently talked about Utility clothing. In November 1941, the government decreed that those manufacturers still permitted to make domestic furniture would only be able to make articles from a specified list of twenty pieces, using only a specified maximum amount of wood in their construction. Definitely not among the twenty pieces of furniture were comfortable deep-sprung sofas and armchairs, which would have required heavy upholstery fabrics and metal springs. A couple of months after it was announced, the already very small timber quota for domestic furniture was cut by one-third; the use of plywood, needed in the building of Mosquito fighter-bombers, was forbidden altogether.

It was Board of Trade officials, not the manufacturers, who decided on the kind of new furniture that people could buy, high-mindedly believing that they should be 'influencing

1941
JUNE

1 17,000 Allied troops are successfully evacuated from Crete.
British re-enter Baghdad and the Regent is reinstated.

2 Ruhr industrial area bombed by RAF.

4 Pro-Allied government installed in Iraq.
Air raid on Alexandria, 100 killed.

7 First of five night raids on Brest by the RAF.

8 Allies invade Syria and Lebanon.

9 British advance 40 miles (64 kilometres) into southern Syria and Lebanon. Occupation of Tyre.

11 RAF raids Rhr, Rhineland and German ports in the first of 20 consecutive night raids.

13 Russo–Japanese trade agreement announced in Tokyo.

14 President Roosevelt orders that all German and Italian assets are to be frozen in the USA.

15 Operation Battleaxe begins in North Africa to relieve Australian-held Tobruk.

16 Roosevelt orders the closure of all German consulates on US territory.

17 Rommel beats back British attack at Sollum.
Operation Battleaxe was a major failure, with 1,000 British casualties and 100 tanks lost.

1941
JUNE

19 Germany and Italy expel US consul officials in retaliation for US moves.

21 Allied troops occupy Damascus.

22 Germany attacks Russia as Operation Barbarossa begins. This was the greatest military offensive in the history of the war.

23 Germans sweep into western Russia, crossing the River Bug.

24 Germans capture Vilna and Kaunas as they move east into Russia.

26 Finland declares war on Russia.
Heavy fighting in Minsk as the Germans continue to advance.

27 Hungary declares war on USSR.

28 Germans capture Minsk.

29 Göring is named as Hitler's successor.

30 Germans advance in Russian- occupied Poland, taking control of Lvov.

It was also during the months of June 1941 that the Nazi SS Einsatzgrüppen began their mass murder.

In order to ensure a fair distribution of the new Utility furniture, the government made it available only to specified 'priority classes' to whom permits were issued. The classes included people who had been bombed-out and newly-weds setting up their first homes; newly-weds moving into in-laws' homes were permitted one or two extra pieces, but not the full range. As well as paying the (government-controlled) purchase price of the furniture, the buyer had also to provide a certain number of units, more for large pieces like a wardrobe, fewer for smaller pieces: a kitchen chair, for instance, could be bought with the purchase price plus just one unit.

Once the Blitz was over and life on the home front settled into a drab austerity, simply obtaining basic consumer goods became very much a matter of being in the right shop at the right time. Certain household basic essentials had to be rationed, to ensure that everyone got at least some of them. Foremost among these was soap, including washing powder, which was rationed in February 1942.

UTILITY FURNISHING FABRICS

Government control of furniture design extended to the fabrics which could be used to cover or upholster it. A small sub-group of the Advisory Committee on Utility Furniture, called the Design Panel, was set up in mid-1943 to advise on the creation of new fabric designs. The splendid geometric sweeps of colour and pattern typical of 1930s Art Deco design were out. Instead, the first two designs, called 'Skelda' and 'Flora', which were introduced in 1944, had small patterns with a repeat of only 3–4 inches (7–10 centimetres), so as to reduce fabric wastage to a minimum. Fabric weight was low and colour choice small – only rust, green, blue and cream (natural) were available.

▶ *Furniture Factory*
Women making utility furniture, which will only be available by permit.

▲ *Hanging Up Washing*
30 April 1941: Members of the WVS hanging up washing that has been collected and washed by the mobile clothes-washing service, which operates self-contained Rinso units (background) for bomb-damaged households in east and south London.

The type of soap powder available to housewives became markedly inferior and manufacturers, such as the makers of Rinso, officially a 'No. 1 soap powder', published adverts advising people on how best to use it. 'You don't need to boil', said a 1944 Rinso ad, 'you simply soak . . . [using the] wartime method, half the water and two-thirds the Rinso', then you sit back at the end of washday and await the admiration of your husband, sitting in his comfy chair and taking his pipe out of his mouth to tell you that you are 'a marvel, darling, running the house and a job too.' Even in wartime, men seldom took any part in housework.

A series of Limitations of Supplies Orders, the first one in 1940, greatly restricted the production of most consumer goods from pottery and cutlery to toys and games. Some household goods were classed as 'fripperies' and their manufacture was prohibited altogether. Housewives might agree that a birdcage or a coffee percolator was a frippery in wartime, but a vacuum cleaner or a refrigerator? By 1943, when new saucepans were almost unobtainable, housewives, most of whom by now were doing part-time jobs as well as running households, were greatly regretting the generous impulse that had made them give their saucepans to the Spitfire Fund back in 1940.

▲ *Pots For War Effort*
A Chelsea Pensioner adds a frying pan to a heap of aluminium
pots and pans at the WVS depot at Chelsea, following Lord
Beaverbrook's appeal for aluminium for the war effort.

1941
JULY

1 Germans take Baltic port of Riga.
Daylight offensives by RAF begin over Northern France, Channel and Occupied Europe.

2 USSR attacked by German, Romanian and Hungarian troops in the south.

3 Stalin calls for a 'scorched earth' policy.

4 British Community party backs the war after officially dropping its peace campaign.

7 US troops set up a garrison in Iceland.

8 Soviet President Litninov broadcasts from Moscow in English, stating that the UK and Russia must stand up against Germany together.

9 Germans defeat Russians at Minsk.

10 Germans cross the River Dnieper in the Ukraine and also urge Japan to enter the war.
Finnish Karelian Army invades Russia.

12 Mutual Assistance Agreement signed between Britain and Russia.
First German air raid on Moscow.

14 British occupy Syria.

15 Empire forces enter Beirut.

20 Stalin announces himself as Defence commissar. Russia resumes diplomatic relations with occupied countries.

THE FOOD FRONT

In the 1930s, much of Britain's food came from abroad, shipped in from most of the countries of the Empire, from North and South America and from Europe.

Another war in Europe that inevitably involved shipping in the world's major seaways would obviously have a catastrophic effect on imports of food into Britain. The British government's advanced planning for war therefore included establishing a Ministry of Food in 1937.

Once war was declared, the Ministry of Food and its minister, Lord Woolton, played ever-growing parts in everyone's lives. Lord Woolton was immortalised in the name of perhaps the most famous recipe to come out of World War II, Woolton Pie. This was a vegetable-based concoction that at its most basic, and without the help of extras like a cheese sauce or cream, was a less than exciting dish.

A constant flow of recipes, including Woolton Pie, and food advice in booklets, leaflets, pamphlets and information adverts called 'Food Facts', featuring such characters as Potato Pete and Doctor Carrot, came from the Ministry's Food Advice Division. Their intention was to keep housewives well-informed about the nutritional value of foods, especially vegetables and fruit, and to offer guidance for preparing interesting meals from the suddenly limited range of foods available. A team of home

THE KITCHEN FRONT

One of the greatest helps to housewives trying to feed families well with limited resources was the BBC Home Service's five-minute programme, The Kitchen Front, broadcast at 8.15 a.m. from Tuesday to Friday throughout the war. The timing, after the 8 o'clock news bulletin, was intended to catch housewives before they went out to do their shopping – which soon involved long hours of queuing. The programme, with contributions from a wide range of people, including the cookery writer Ambrose Heath, Marguerite Patten, the actresses Elsie and Doris Waters and even Lord Woolton himself, soon attracted a large audience; within a couple of weeks of the first programme 30,000 people had written in asking for recipes.

◀ *The Price Of Sugar*
27 September 1939: A London shopkeeper puts up a sign announcing the new price of sugar as revealed in the Budget. The price has risen by a penny a pound.

1941
JULY

26 Roosevelt freezes Japanese assets in the USA and suspends relations.
Italians attack Valetta harbour in Malta, destroying eight boats.

27 Japanese occupy bases in Indo-China.
First air raid on London for ten weeks.

28 40,000 Japanese troops land in Indo-China and Japan freezes US and UK assets.

29 Marshal Shukov resigns as Russian Chief of Staff.

30 US forces seize 17 Japanese spy fishing boats in Hawaiian waters.

31 Göring instructs Heydrich to prepare for the 'Final Solution'.

AUGUST

1 Roosevelt announces an oil embargo against aggressor states.

5 Romanians commence 73-day siege of the port of Odessa in the Black Sea.
310,000 Soviets captured after fighting ends around Smolensk.

7 US Senate extends its National Service to 30 months.
Russian aircraft bomb Berlin.

14 Roosevelt and Churchill sign the Atlantic Charter.

18 Russians withdraw across the Dnieper River.

economists, including the redoubtable Marguerite Patten, still one of Britain's leading cookery writers, carried on the Food Advice Division's work through Food Advice Centres, which were set up all over the country.

The Ministry of Food's greatest task during the war and for nearly a decade after it was to oversee the fair distribution and rationing of basic essential foods. Food rationing, which was introduced in January 1940, was organised by the Ministry through 1,300 local offices throughout the country.

Rationing of basic foods was brought in gradually, starting with bacon, ham, sugar and butter in January 1940. In March, meat was rationed and in July tea, margarine, cooking fat and cheese. In March 1941, jam, marmalade, treacle and syrup were all rationed and in June the distribution of eggs was controlled, as was, in November, the distribution of milk. The last of the war-time rationing came in July 1942, when sweets were put on the ration list.

The eggs available on the ration were often not whole eggs, but dried egg powder, sold in packs or tins. Quite a lot of this notoriously difficult to use, much-disliked product came from the United States. Dried egg was pure egg with all its moisture removed. In some recipes, the egg powder could be spooned straight from the tin, but for most cooking purposes it had to be reconstituted; one level tablespoon of dried egg powder mixed with two tablespoons of water gave a mixture that was the equivalent of one fresh egg.

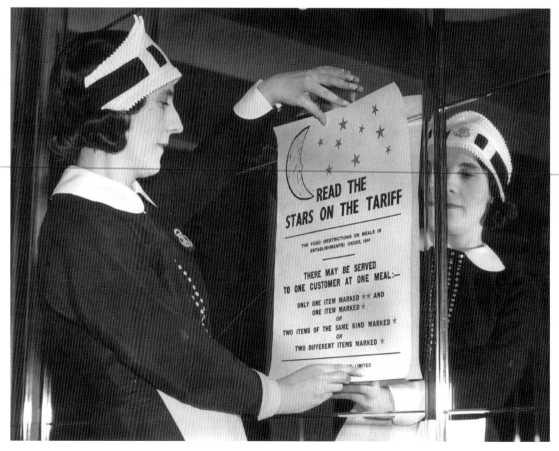

A complicated system of ration books, coupons and points controlled the distribution of rations through food shops. Every person in the country had a ration book, containing on its front cover the same details about the person that was on his or her identity card. Ration books could only be used at retailers whose names and addresses were listed in it (and who kept in their shops counterfoils of the list in the book). Of course, it could be said, that rationing had its good points too, because it meant that everybody got their fair share of what was available. For people in the lower income bracket, it meant that they were getting more food during the war than before. People were better educated about food, as the government campaigned for the public to eat more vegetables. They also provided cod liver oil and orange juice for children. Things like fish were never rationed, as they were virtually unobtainable and, if they were on sale, the queues were so long that

◀ *Ration Menu*
10 March 1941: A 'nippy' waitress at a Lyons' teashop puts up a poster to explain the new rationing system, which ranks scarce food according to stars. Customers may only have one item with two stars or two items with one star.

1941
AUGUST

20 German siege of Leningrad begins.
21 First Arctic convoy leaves Iceland for Russia.
25 British and Russian troops invade Iran.
26 German losses on Russian Front mount to 440,000, more than in the entire war before 22 June.
29 Iranian government orders a ceasefire.
Russians evacuate Karelian Isthmus to Leningrad.
30 Germans cut the last rail link between Leningrad and the remainder of the USSR.

AN ADULT'S WEEKLY RATIONS

Although the amounts varied slightly, depending on availability, the following amounts were what one adult could expect to have of the rationed foods each week:
Bacon and ham – 4oz (100g);
Meat – 1 shilling and 2 pennies (6 pence)-worth of what was available; sausages were not rationed, but were rarely seen, and offal was sometimes part of the ration;
Butter and cheese – 2oz (50g), although sometimes 4 oz (100g) and even 8oz (225g) of cheese was available;
Margarine and cooking fat – 4oz (100g), sometimes only 2oz (50g) of the latter;
Milk – 3 pints (1800ml), sometimes dropping to 2 pints (1200ml); 'Household' milk, which was skimmed or dried milk, was sometimes available as 1 packet every 4 weeks;
Sugar – 8oz (225g), which had to cover baking and jam-making as well as one's cup of tea, although, if it was available, extra sugar would be issued at jam-making times;
Preserves – 1lb (450g) every 2 months;
Tea – 2oz (50g);
Eggs – 1 whole egg, if available, but sometimes dropping to 1 every 2 weeks; the dried egg ration was 1 packet every 4 weeks;
Sweets – 12oz (350g each 4 weeks.

▲ *Milk Mountain*
17 November 1941: Twelve million tins of powdered milk from North America and New Zealand being stacked in cardboard boxes ready for distribution in Britain during World War II.

orange juice, that children were allocated. (Children were helped in other ways, oranges, for instance, when available being kept solely for children until they had been in the greengrocer's display for five days.)

As well as the coupons, there was a monthly points system giving 16 points that could be spent on 'extras'; one can of fish or meat or 2lb (900g) of dried fruit, for example, would use up all 16 points, whereas only one point (plus the 8d/3½ pence purchase price) would get the housewife an 8oz (250g) packet of Krisvita Crispbread. The British people were finally able to tear up their ration books in June 1954, when meat was the last food to come off the ration.

people had to wait for hours with no promise of what they were getting when they reached the front.

The ration book was designed to show exactly when and how many coupons had been used to purchase the various rationed foods. Children's ration books, called R.B.2, included spaces for the extra foods, such as

1941
SEPTEMBER

1 Nazis order that all Jews must wear a yellow star.
2 First experimental use of gas chambers at Auschwitz.
15 Siege of Leningrad begins.
16 Shah of Iran abdicates and Crown Prince takes over.
19 Germans take Kiev.
24 First U-boat enters the Mediterranean.
26 German High Command records the capture of 655,000 prisoners in Kiev.
29 Babi Yar massacre – Germans kill nearly 34,000 Jews at Kiev.
30 General Guderian with the German Army opens Moscow Drive.

▲ *Tinned Food*
29 November 1941: A shop assistant arranges newly arrived tinned meats from the United States, as part of the 'lease-lend' agreement.

While the Ministry of Food was in the forefront of giving advice about optimum use of the foods available, the Ministry of Agriculture was the government department responsible for the production of as much food as possible in wartime Britain. By the late 1930s, after nearly twenty years of cheap imports of food, especially diary products, meat, cereals, fats, sugar and fruit, British agriculture was very much given over to pasture. This would have to change – and rapidly.

The Emergency Powers Act gave the Ministry of Agriculture the power, often used with draconian thoroughness, to make that change. Throughout the war, the Ministry of Agriculture, working through War Agriculture Committees (soon referred to as 'War Ags') set up in every county, directed and controlled the production of the food that fed the nation.

A 'Ploughing-Up' campaign, begun in the spring of 1939, persuaded farmers (with an incentive payment of £2 an acre) to switch from growing animal feed on grassland to growing grains such as oats, wheat and barley and vegetables like potatoes and sugar beet for human consumption instead. The Ministry of Agriculture hoped that by harvest time in 1940 there would be an additional 1.7 million acres of farmland devoted to growing food. Farmers, many of them using horse-drawn tractors and ploughs because of petrol rationing, had achieved this change several months before that date.

While this was going on, the War Ags also tried to bring into production as much hitherto unproductive land in their counties as they could, including marshland, barren hillsides, scrubland ignored for centuries and much else. The mechanisation of farming

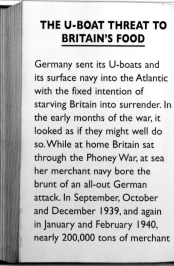

► *Chicken Woman*
1941: One of many women taking up farming jobs during the war. Miss Marshall collects eggs from chickens in Worcestershire.

THE U-BOAT THREAT TO BRITAIN'S FOOD

Germany sent its U-boats and its surface navy into the Atlantic with the fixed intention of starving Britain into surrender. In the early months of the war, it looked as if they might well do so. While at home Britain sat through the Phoney War, at sea her merchant navy bore the brunt of an all-out German attack. In September, October and December 1939, and again in January and February 1940, nearly 200,000 tons of merchant shipping were sunk, with their cargoes, each month. These figures, so bad that the government suppressed them, got even worse later in the year, with over 500,000 tons of merchant navy convoys going to the bottom of the ocean in June 1940. This loss of vital food and other supplies, running at about 400,000 tons a month well into 1941, was compounded by the loss of several large European food sources, sucked into the Axis powers' war machine.

◄ *Land Army Fashion*
Two Land Army girls carrying pitchforks
and sporting straw hats to go with their
dungarees. Their carthorse however has no
hat.

gathered pace during the war, as did the use of fertilisers. By the time of the last full wartime harvest, that of 1944, Britain was able to feed itself for 160 days a year – forty days more than in 1939.

It was not just the farmers who fed Britain during the war, they were helped by some 36,000 Land Girls who were pitched into agriculture from the civilian life of offices, beauty salons, department stores and domestic service. Every local authority with a park or public garden or land that could be turned into allotments, every householder with land at the back or front of the house was urged to 'Grow More' and 'Dig for Victory'.

The Ministry of Agriculture's allotment scheme allowed local councils to make use of every piece of land not in full use that they could borrow or rent at an agreed agricultural rent from its owner or occupier. The land was turned into allotments that the government hoped would be taken up by people without gardens of their own and used to grow vegetables and fruit.

In November 1939, the ministry had asked for half a million people to come forward and take up an allotment. In September 1940, by which time

DIGGING FOR VICTORY

One of the most famous slogans of World War II, 'Dig for Victory' was first used in London's *Evening Standard* newspaper, in a leader pushing the government's Grow More campaign. Its succinct mixture of practicality and patriotism made 'Dig for Victory' the perfect propaganda slogan, and the Ministry of Agriculture was quick to pick it up. Its first official use was on a leaflet issued in November 1939, calling for people to take up an allotment. Within a year, Dig for Victory had become a full-blown campaign in its own right, often promoted side by side with the Grow More campaign, and much used in the advertising of food-related products.

▲ *Dig For Victory*
1941: A woman tending to her vegetables on her allotment at Hampstead Heath.

1941

OCTOBER

2 Operation Typhoon begins, which is the German advance on Moscow.

12 Bryansk falls to Germans; women and children evacuated from Moscow.

16 Odessa falls to the Romanians after Soviet evacuation by sea. Japanese government falls and Konoye replaced by Tojo.

18 Germans now only 65 miles (105 km) from Moscow.

19 Stalin declares state of siege in capital with orders to defend their city to the last.

20 50 hostages are shot in Nantes, France, in retaliation for the assassination of German military commander.

24 Germans take Kharkov.

29 Germans advance into Crimea.

30 Germans reach Sevastopol.

31 US destroyer *Reuben James* sunk off Iceland.

NOVEMBER

13 British aircraft carrier *Ark Royal* is sunk off Gibraltar by a U-boat.

18 Operation Crusader, the British offensive in Libya commences.

20 Germans take Rostov.

27 Russian troops retake Rostov.

▲ Firemen's Pigs
The Wyse Pig Club – firemen at an AFS (Auxiliary Fire Service) station in south-west London
with some of the pigs they are raising as part of the war effort.

the Dig for Victory and Grow More campaigns, backed up by dozens of posters and leaflets, were in full cry, the government asked for another 500,000 people to take them on. By this time, Defence Regulations had been amended to allow allotment holders to keep hens, rabbits and pigs on their allotments. Within a couple of years, it was estimated that more than half the country's manual workers were growing food in allotments or gardens.

Many suburban garden lawns were ploughed up and flower beds dug over, to be replaced by vegetable plots, herbs and fruit bushes. Even the Anderson shelter was brought into use in the wartime garden, marrows and other vegetables being grown on its curved, earth-covered roof and mushrooms and rhubarb in its damp interior. Room was also found in many back gardens for a hen run, for ducks and rabbits and even for pigs.

With bacon being rationed, the pig, which could be kept quite easily in a back-garden sty, came to occupy a large part in many a garden-owner's 'grow more' thinking. A Pig Keepers Club, with nearly 7,000 local offshoots, was set up to give people advice on keeping pigs, not just in the back garden but at the back of office blocks and in factory and other workplace yards as well. Pig-swill bins, into which people put every scrap of food waste that could not be used in the home, appeared on many street corners. Local councils had the job of emptying the pig-swill bins and cooking the swill for at least an hour to kill germs and toxins before allowing it to be used as pig feed.

While it was fine for workplace pig clubs or the policemen at Hyde Park station in London to keep pigs (fattened on scraps from the local big hotels in the case of the Hyde Park station pigs) and kill and replace them with a new litter every six months or so, despatching the animals in the back yard could be a major problem for families, especially if the animals in question had become family pets. At least with hens, this dreadful end could be put off for a long time, during which the hens provided the family – and local people – with a supply of fresh eggs.

The availability of fresh eggs dominated the thinking of housewives at all levels of society. Vita Sackville-West, creator of one of England's loveliest gardens at Sissinghurst in Kent,

1941
DECEMBER

5 German attack on Moscow is abandoned.

7 Japanese attack Pearl Harbor.
Hitler issues the 'Night and Fog' decree.

8 USA and Britain declare war on Japan.

10 Siege of Tobruk finally ended. British battleship *Prince of Wales* and battlecruiser *Repulse* sunk by Japanese off coast of Malaysia.

11 Italy and Germany declare war on the USA.

16 Rommel begins a retreat to El Agheila in North Africa.

19 Hitler takes complete command of the German Army.
Japanese land in Hong Kong and British evacuate Penang.

22 Japanese launch main invasion of Philippines.
32,000 Jews killed by Germans in Lithuania.

25 Hong Kong surrenders after a 17-day siege.
British retake Benghazi.
Over 3,000 starve to death in Leningrad.

▲ *Woman's Work*
Women employed in steel mills enjoying a
smoke during a short break. During WW II
they kept the mills operating. Safety wear
includes a hood, goggles, a leather apron
and gloves.

mentioned eggs in *Vogue* magazine in July 1943: 'Perhaps country-dwellers are better off than town-dwellers. The egg problem, for instance, isn't so acute, because most of them keep a few hens. The price and staleness of vegetables doesn't worry them, because they grow their own . . .' Vita Sackville-West was right in that throughout the war it was much easier for people with the space of the countryside or large country gardens around them to grow more and to dig for victory than it was for people in urban areas.

Not all food was eaten at home, of course, and the Ministry of Food was soon having a big say in the business of eating out, beginning with eating at work. Well aware that properly fed workers were healthier workers, the government early in the war made it compulsory for factories to install workers' canteens. By the end of 1944, there were 30,500 canteens in workplaces all over the country.

The canteens were kept supplied with the raw ingredients for nutritious meals, with plenty of tea and, in factories with more than 200 employees, cigarettes as well. The cigarettes were another piece of positive lateral thinking by Lord Beaverbrook. He noticed that many workers in Sheffield's hard-pressed factories, when they heard that cigarettes were available in the city, took time off to queue for them. He persuaded the government to release supplies of precious American Lend-Lease Virginia leaf cigarettes to larger factories, where they were sold at a rate of forty cigarettes per worker per week.

During the Blitz, when so many people were bombed out of their homes or their cooking facilities were damaged or destroyed, Communal Feeding Centres were set up. Soon re-named, at Winston Churchill's suggestion, the more attractive British Restaurants, these unpretentious eating places were open to everyone. Supplied with otherwise hard-to-obtain cookers, pots and pans, crockery and cutlery by the Ministry of Food, British Restaurants provided more than adequate meals at very low prices – 1d for a bowl of lentil soup, 6d or 8d for a main course of rabbit pie and vegetables, 2d for sultana roll or rice pudding, and whole meals for children for 4d – for thousands of people up and down the country throughout the war. Although their number never reached the 10,000 the government had hoped for, by 1944 there were enough British Restaurants to serve an average of 600,000 meals a day in the towns and cities of Britain.

The government ensured that schoolchildren were properly fed by providing school meals. By February 1945, Britain's schools were dishing up 1,850,000 meals every day. There was even some help for workers in the fields, though this was limited because of the rationing of petrol, and the WVS managed to operate a few of their mobile canteens in country areas.

At the top end of the scale, grand hotels and restaurants flourished in the early years of the war. Since most of the expensive foods and drinks that made up their menus were not rationed, they were available to anyone prepared to pay for them. And many people were. As the diarist and politician Sir Henry 'Chips' Channon noted in his diary in

1942
JANUARY

1 Declaration of the United Nations signed by 26 Allied nations.
13 Germans begin a U-boat offensive along east coast of the USA.
20 SS Leader Heydrich, announces 'Final solution of Jewish problem' to the Wannsee Conference.
21 Rommel's counter-offensive from El Agheila begins.
26 First American forces arrive in Great Britain.
29 Rommel recaptures Benghazi.
30 British withdraw to Singapore Island with Japanese only 18 miles (29 km) away.

FEBRUARY

1 Puppet government set up in Norway under the treacherous Quisling.
3 Japanese air raids on Port Moresby.
4 Japanese bomb Singapore for four days non-stop.
14 Japanese invasion of Sumatra begins.
17 Japanese invade Bali and bomb Darwin, Australia.
27 Battle of the Java Sea for three days Allies lose five cruisers and six destroyers.

ORDERED EATING

Among the government directives covering eating out in wartime, the Meals in Establishments Order 1942 dictated what diners could choose to eat in restaurants. The menu card for VE Day, 8 May 1945, at Simpson's-in-the-Strand in London explained it: 'By the terms of this Order it is not permissible to serve or consume more than three courses at any meal; nor may any person have at a meal more than one dish marked * [meat and fish dishes] and one dish marked § [egg and vegetable main courses], or alternatively, two dishes marked §. Dishes unmarked may be ordered instead of those marked, or in addition to them, provided that the limit of three courses is not exceeded, nor the maximum permitted price [5 shillings, or 25 pence].'

▲ *Mobile Food*
circa 1942: A mobile canteen stopping in a London street to offer people hot meals.

November 1940, there must have been a thousand people on the dance floor of the Dorchester Hotel the night he dined there with friends. 'London lives well: I have never seen more lavishness, more money spent, or more food consumed than tonight.... The contrast between the light and gaiety within, and the blackout and roaring guns outside was terrific....'

Such lavishness and high-living caused considerable resentment among the ordinary population, many of whom felt that people should pay with their ration coupons for food in restaurants, just as they paid for it in shops. A Gallup Poll in early 1941, drawing attention to this growing resentment at the obvious inequality between the rich and the less well-off as far as food and diet went, prodded the government into taking action. There was not a lot they could do, although the Ministry of Food did try to get a grip on things by putting an upper limit on the price of meals and on the number of courses that could be served during a meal. But there was no way of stopping people eating two or three meals in two or three different restaurants in one day, should they so wish.

▲ *Business as Usual*
Signs outside small restaurant proclaiming WE ARE CARRYING ON!
HITLER WILL NOT BEAT US show the efforts of most Londoners to
maintain a semblance of normalcy throughout the ongoing German air raid
attacks on the city, one of which is taking place as this picture is snapped.

KEEPING UP APPEARANCES

Where the Ministry of Food was, appropriately enough, in charge of ensuring that the nation was adequately fed during the war, it was the Board of Trade, the government department in charge of trade and business, that dictated, in an increasingly draconian manner, the style, shape and fabric content of the clothes bought during the war and for nearly four years after it by every man, woman and child in the country.

Although people accepted that clothing fabrics would be in short supply, it still came as a shock to many when clothing was actually rationed, like food. When the President of the Board of Trade announced immediate clothes rationing on 1 June 1941, the reason given was to 'provide fair distribution of available supplies'. But the government was also intent, not only on reducing consumer spending, but also on cutting the numbers of workers tied up in clothing textile manufacture when they could have been more usefully employed in war production. Clothes rationing in Britain did not end until 1949.

To prevent hoarding, price rises and the development of a 'black market', clothes rationing was kept a closely guarded secret until it was announced. Thus, no clothing coupons or ration books were ready printed in June 1941, and people were instructed to use twenty-six 'spare' margarine coupons in their food ration books instead. These would be the first instalment of the sixty-six coupons that everyone would have in the first fifteen months of rationing – sufficient, the government calculated, for the purchase of about half of the average amount of clothing a person bought before the war.

It was a year before the first clothes ration books were issued. They contained sixty coupons, intended to last until the end of July 1943, but, in the event, were all that was allocated until the beginning of September 1943, when the allocation dropped to 40 coupons (it rose again to 48 coupons in 1944). In September 1945, with the war over, the allocation dropped down to a mere 36 coupons a year, largely because of a serious shortage of workers in the nation's textile mills.

The fact that the clothing ration coupons came in three different colours, green, brown and red, intended to cover use by numerous different categories of people, including workers, such as miners, with special clothing needs, expectant mothers, new babies and 'certain older children' who might be growing too big for children's clothes (who should decide this?), was a sign that clothes rationing was not going to be simple. And, indeed, it turned out to be nightmarishly complicated, so much so that the government had to issue a booklet, called *The Clothing Quiz*, to help people understand the system.

LOST RATION BOOKS

Losing a clothes ration book was a serious thing. A book lost in a bombing could be replaced by the local Assistance Board, but any other loss, unless 'exceptional need' could be proved, probably meant the replacement was unlikely. In the early months of clothes rationing, people were recompensed for the 'loss' of food or clothing ration books with loose coupons – something like 27,000,000 during the first year. But the system was so abused that the Board of Trade cracked down on the use of loose coupons, brought in a complex coupon banking system, and ruled that only coupons in books were acceptable in shops. It even employed its own snoopers, who visited clothing shops trying to buy clothes with loose coupons.

◀ *Clothes Rationing*
A couple of holidaymakers reading about clothes rationing in a newspaper.

1942
MARCH

1 Allies abandon Java and head for Australia.
7 Large-scale Japanese landings on the island of New Guinea and Rangoon falls to the Japanese.
17 MacArthur appointed Supreme Commander, South West Pacific.
18 Lord Mountbatten appointed Chief of Combined Operations.
22 Three-day battle begins in the Mediterranean.
25 British government suffers first defeat of the war in Grantham by-election as Independent win.
28 St Nazaire raid to occupied France.

APRIL

3 2,000 killed in Japanese bombing of Mandalay
9 78,000 US–Filipino troops are captured on Bataan.
10 'Death March' of captured US–Filipino troops.
18 First US air raid on Tokyo and Japan by sixteen B-25 bombers led by Colonel Doolittle.
23 German air raids begin against cathedral cities in Britain.
24 Luftwaffe begin Baedeker raids on historic cities in Britain.
30 British retreat over the Irrawaqddy completed at Mandalay.

1942
MAY

4 USA begins food rationing. Battle of the Coral Sea, first naval clash fought entirely with naval aircraft.

5 British forces take Diego Suarez in Vichy-held Madagascar, converting it into an air and naval base against the Japanese.

6 On Corregidor, US General Jonathan Wainwright surrenders his forces – 15,000 US and Filipino soldiers – to the Japanese.

8 Battle of the Coral Sea ends as a tactical victory for the Japanese.

12 Soviet Army launch their first major offensive of the war and took Khartov in the eastern Ukraine from the Germans.
1,500 Jews gassed in Auschwitz.

14 Women's Auxiliary Army Corps is established.

18 Allied forces bomb the harbour city of Kupang, Timor.

26 Battle of Gazala. Tank battle at Bir Hakein – African corps vs. British army.

27 SS General Reinhard Heydrich critically wounded in Prague by Czech commandos.

29 Bing Crosby records Irving Berlin's 'White Christmas' in Los Angeles for Decca Records.

30 RAF bomb Cologne in first of 1,000 bomber night raids.

▲ *Clothing Rations*
A woman using her clothes ration book to buy underwear at Woolworths.

The Board of Trade's clothes rationing lists attempted to include most items of clothing that the British man, women and child might wish to buy, for both their working and private lives, and were therefore both lengthy and, occasionally, esoteric (for example, leggings, gaiters or

◀ *Cheap Clothes*
A woman wearing a blouse and dungarees, which cost very few ration coupons.

spats, requiring 3 coupons for adults, 2 for children). Coupon requirements included 26 for a man's suit, 18 for a woman's (also the amount for a lined winter coat); a man's shirt took 5 coupons, a woman's cotton or rayon dress 7 coupons (but her winter woollen dress needed 11); men's socks ('half-hose, not woollen, or pair of ankle socks not exceeding eight inches [20 centimetres] from point of heel to top of sock when not turned down') took 1 coupon, a pair of women's stockings (soon very hard to get, anyway), 2 coupons. Babies' knitted booties required half a coupon. One slight relief was that hats did not require coupons.

With these lists beside them, people could work out in advance their clothing purchases

1942

JUNE

1 Germans bomb Canterbury in reprisal for Cologne.

4 Battle of Medway begins. Japan's first major defeat in WWII.
Heydrich dies of his wounds.

5 Siege of Sebastopol begins.

10 Nazis carry out massacre in village of Lidice in reprisal for assassination of Heydrich.

21 Rommel captures Tobruk.

24 Eisenhower appointed commander of US forces in Europe.

25 Eisenhower arrives in London.

30 Rommel reaches El Alamein near Cairo, Egypt.

JULY

1 First Battle of El Alamein.

3 Germans take Sebastopol.

5 Soviet resistance in the Crimea ends.

9 Germans begin a drive towards Stalingrad in the USSR.

22 First deportations from the Warsaw Ghetto to concentration camps.
Treblinka extermination camp is opened.

31 Germans continue to advance into north Caucasus.

for the coming year or so. The foolish blew their allocation early in the summer then found that, come autumn, there were no coupons left for essential winter clothing. Even if people had the right number of coupons, they often found that they simply could not afford the purchase price of the garments they wanted, for the price of clothing rocketed in the early years of the war: a made-to-measure suit, 14 guineas (£14.70) at the start of the war, was soon costing up to £42, and pretty nighties, a delightful present at 25 shillings (£1.25) became something to consider very seriously when their price reached £12 or more.

Nor was buying second-hand clothes a simple option, unless from private dealers, because the second-hand clothing trade was soon enmeshed in a complex formula for working out if and how many coupons were needed in addition to the retail price. Nor could you, following Scarlett O'Hara's way of dealing with a depleted wartime wardrobe in the hugely popular film *Gone With the Wind*, easily make yourself clothes out of curtain material, because furnishing fabrics, like dress fabrics, were rationed and therefore needed precious coupons to buy.

The Board of Trade decided to use clothing as the trading sector in which it would first use the concept of wartime 'utility' standards in the making of good-quality products that could be sold at a reasonable price. 'Utility' was, perhaps, not a good word to choose for this exercise in government control of public style and taste, for it suggested a dreary economy. In fact, as with Utility furniture, which came in a few months later, Utility clothing, announced in the Civilian Clothing Order of June 1942 and first shown to the public in a special display of thirty-two garments in September, turned out to be rather good. Even *Vogue* approved of the styles and fabrics on show – as well the magazine might, since the Board of Trade had called in ideas from eight of the leading dress designers of the day, including two Royal Family favourites, Norman Hartnell and Hardy Amies.

▲ *Utility Clothing*
Models at Bush House, London, displaying clothes made from government utility materials, at the first mixed mannequin show ever held.

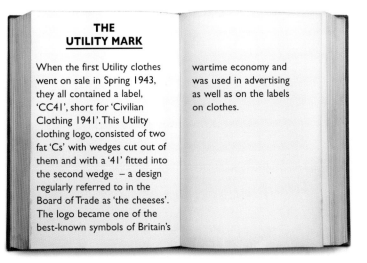

THE UTILITY MARK

When the first Utility clothes went on sale in Spring 1943, they all contained a label, 'CC41', short for 'Civilian Clothing 1941'. This Utility clothing logo, consisted of two fat 'Cs' with wedges cut out of them and with a '41' fitted into the second wedge – a design regularly referred to in the Board of Trade as 'the cheeses'. The logo became one of the best-known symbols of Britain's wartime economy and was used in advertising as well as on the labels on clothes.

1942
AUGUST

4 Germans begin final drive for Stalingrad.
7 British General Montgomery takes command of the Eighth Army in North Africa.
9 Battle of Savo Island.
12 Stalin and Churchill meet in Moscow.
17 First all-American air attack in Europe.
23 Massive German air raid on Stalingrad.
30 Battle of Alam Halfa – Rommel sustains heavy losses.

SEPTEMBER

2 Rommel driven back by Montgomery in the Battle of Alam Halfa.
3 Fierce desert battle as RAF and New Zealand soldiers attack Axis supply lines.
13 Battle of Stalingrad begins.

OCTOBER

5 German eyewitness reports SS mass murder.
7 UN Commission to investigate war crimes announced in London and Washington.
11 Battle of Cape Esperance.
18 Hitler orders the execution of all captured British commandos.
23 Second Battle of El Alamein begins.
26 Battle of Santa Cruz – US attack large Japanese fleet.

▲ *Home-Made Jackets*
Beat wartime rationing by making your own clothes, for example, simple skin jackets with knitted sleeves.

The Board of Trade, when planning the regulations for the Utility clothing scheme, decided that only four basic outfits should be available – a top coat and a suit, in both men's and women's styles, and, for women, an afternoon dress and a cotton overall dress. The rules governing their manufacture were strict, and were based on using as little fabric as possible. Suits and coats, which could not be double-breasted, had narrow lapels, men's trousers were made without turnups, and women's skirts were all made to the same (shortish) length, regardless of the fact that British women were not all the same height. Numbers of buttons and pockets were restricted and embroidery or lace trimmings were forbidden. The cut of the garments was practical, pared-down and almost military in outline – and thus very much in tune with the wartime mood.

The limited availability of new clothing made looking after the contents of one's existing wardrobe of huge importance. 'Make Do and Mend' and 'Sew and Save' became two more additions to Britain's growing list of wartime slogans. In fact, making do and mending became everyone's patriotic duty, although many women must have thought that the President of the Board of Trade, Hugh Dalton, was going a bit far when he told the readers of *Good House-keeping* magazine in August 1943 that 'to

▲ *Darning Socks*
Evacuees darning socks at Baron's Estate, Hampshire.

1942

NOVEMBER

1 Operation Supercharge (Allies break Axis lines at El Alamein).
8 Operation Torch begins in North West Africa.
11 Germans and Italians invade unoccupied Vichy, France.
13 First sea battle of Guadalcanal.
19 Soviet counter-offensive at Stalingrad begins.
27 German troops enter Toulon.
30 Battle of Tassafaronga.

DECEMBER

1 Raids on Bordeau harbour.
2 Professor Enrico Fermi sets up an atomic reactor in Chicago.
13 Rommel begins retreat from El Agheila.
16 Soviets defeat Italian troops on the River Don in the USSR.
17 Final US–Australian assault on Buna begins.
British Foreign Secretary Eden tells the House of Commons of mass executions of Jews by Nazis. USA declares those war crimes will be avenged.
20 Japanese bomb Calcutta for the first time.
24 USA bombs Wake Island.
27 General Giraud becomes leader of French Africa.
31 Battle of the Barents Sea between German and British fleets.

wear clothes that have been patched and darned – perhaps many times – is to show oneself a true patriot. The "right" clothes are those we have worn for years, and the wrong ones those we buy, when we don't absolutely need them'.

Making do with the clothes one already had involved the use of considerable ingenuity, displayed by homemakers and manufacturers alike. Darning, patching and repairing everything from precious silk stockings to one's husband's trousers became, if not a patriotic duty, then certainly a way of life.

Manufacturers did help, producing special trouser-bottom protectors, for instance, or offering a service whereby last year's winter coat could be turned into this year's stylish suit, for a price that did not need to include precious clothing coupons.

Many women also became adept at re-using fabric to sew new clothes on their carefully maintained pre-war sewing machines. Because knitting wool, like dress fabrics, was soon in short supply (and both were rationed, anyway), it became a regular job to unpick old hand-knitted garments and re-use the wool to knit something that looked new and smart: the wartime fashion for striped knitwear grew out of the practice of using old knitting wools together with a few balls of new wool.

Women's magazines, too, although much reduced in size and page extent because of paper rationing, continued throughout the war to help boost morale by offering women much useful and often wonderfully imaginative advice on eking out and making do with the contents of their family's wardrobes.

A theme common to most women's magazines was that it was their readers' patriotic duty to look smart, not just for themselves but for their menfolk returning from the war. *Good Housekeeping* emphasised the theme through many articles covering everything from turning elderly fur coats into warm waistcoats or slip-coats (and using the bits left over for fur collars and mitts) and titivating hats or making 'becoming turbans' with a yard of jersey fabric to making 'cheerful sleeveless pullovers' to 'spice up tired frocks'. At the same time, the magazine did not allow their

▲ *Clothes Exchange*
To extend the clothes rationing system the Women's Voluntary Service have set up a depot where children's clothes can be exchanged.

readers to mis-use their clothing coupons, regularly reminding them how long the current allocation of coupons had to last (usually for a dispiriting number of months ahead).

Another women's magazines theme was the importance of keeping up appearances in wartime. Having your hair permanently waved, for instance, was not considered frivolous; rather, it was a necessity for women doing war work to keep 'the hair always neat and

LIPSTICK, HOME FRONT STYLE

Lipstick had become an important part of a woman's make-up armoury during the 1930s, when lipgloss, lipstick with a sun-protection factor, lipstick brushes and clever click-top, spring-operated lipstick cases all appeared for the first time. Wartime Limitations of Supplies orders meant that lipstick manufacture, a slow process as lipstick was still made by hand, was cut to a minimum. By 1944, when a lipstick machine was available (it made only 144 lipsticks at a time), lipsticks were being sold in wooden holders to conserve metal. Many women made do with petroleum jelly ('Vaseline') as a lipgloss.

pretty', as one perm solution manufacturer put it in a women's magazine advert. And, as *Vogue* put it at the height of the war, 'during World War II it becomes female citizens' patriotic duty to "put their face on", encouraged by the film industry. This gives lipstick respectability.'

To give Hugh Dalton and the Board of Trade their due, they recognised that it was essential to keep up the morale of Britain's women in wartime and tried to make essential cosmetics, perm solutions and the like available – sometimes. But anything of a 'cosmetic' nature, whether women's lipsticks, rouges and vanishing creams, or men's razors and razor blades, were always in short supply, and people got used to keeping an eagle eye on the contents of shop shelves or of keeping an ear open for rumours in pubs and streets about things being 'available', often in street markets or, almost as often, 'round the back of the pub' or on the 'black market'.

Women found many ingenious substitutes for scarce cosmetics. Boot polish replaced mascara on many dressing tables, although dark-lashed women used Vaseline to give their lashes a thickening gloss. Beetroot juice reddened lips and rose petals steeped in red wine for several weeks were used as a substitute for rouge.

As for those precious pre-war silk stockings, well, clever lateral thinking and illusion had to replace them – even after the G.I.s arrived from North America with their miraculous nylons. Tan-coloured creams were painted over legs, and a brown line was drawn up the back of each leg to give the impression that the legs' owner was wearing stockings. Enterprising beauticians set up leg-painting booths where women could have 'stockings painted on their legs' in the shade of their choice for 3d [just over 1p] a leg.

The stocking crisis was such that the Church of England eventually issued a statement saying that it was perfectly acceptable for women to come to church without wearing stockings or hats. Thus another step along the road of social revolution was taken in wartime Britain.

▲ *Slipper Gift*
Woollen slippers were ideal for Christmas presents because they could be made at home without the need for using rationed coupons.

▲ *Painting Legs*
During stocking rationing, a beautician at the newly opened
Bare Leg Beauty Bar at Kennard's store in Croydon paints
stockings onto a customer's skin.

1943
JANUARY

2/3 Germans begin to withdraw from Caucasus.

10 Soviets begin an offensive against the Germans in Stalingrad.

14/ Casablanca conference
24 between Churchill and Roosevelt.
Roosevelt announces that the war can only end with an unconditional surrender from Germany.

23 Montgomery's Eighth Army takes Tripoli.

27 First bombing raid by USA on Germans at Wilhelmshaven.

FEBRUARY

2 Germans surrender at Stalingrad in the first big defeat of Hitler's armies.

8 Soviet troops take Kursk.

14 Battle of Kasserine Pass between the US First Armoured Division and German Panzers in North Africa.

16 Soviets retake Kharkov.

18 Nazis arrest White Rose resistance leaders in Munich.

22 Allies make a commando raid on Myebon.

25 RAF begin round-the-clock bombing in Tunisia.

26 Attack launched by Germans at Medjez el Bab in Tunisia to try and gain ground.

28 Commando raid ruins German atomic weapon plant at Telemark in Norway.

THE ARTS & ENTERTAINMENT IN WARTIME

Of the many regulations issued in the days after war was declared, few were as dismaying to everyone as the one which announced that 'All cinemas, dance halls and places of public entertainment will be closed until further notice' and that 'football matches and outdoor meetings of all kinds which bring large numbers together are prohibited until further notice.'

Just about the only public 'entertainment' left to an already distressed and deeply worried nation were – apart from those museums and art galleries that chose to keep most of their holdings on display – pubs and the BBC's one remaining on-air radio station, which was the Home Service.

Once it was seen that Britain was not going to be subjected to pre-invasion mass bombing, these dreadfully morale-deflating restrictions on public entertainment were relaxed. By mid-September 1939, places of public entertainment, museums and art galleries were open again and a football programme was under way.

In the long run, outdoor events suffered more restrictions than those entertainments that took place indoors. Men could only 'go

to the dogs' at weekends because, in order to prevent people taking time off work, mid-week greyhound racing was forbidden. Horse racing suffered from petrol rationing, which curtailed people's ability to get to race courses, and many sports had their playing fields and other facilities requisitioned. Tennis fans had to accept the courts at Wimbledon being used by the Home Guard; even worse, the hallowed Oval cricket ground in London briefly became a POW camp.

Football, like greyhound racing, became a daytime-only activity, the floodlighting of sports grounds clearly being out of bounds for the duration. By October, football matches – initially a programme of friendly matches with crowds limited to 15,000 in 'safe' areas and to 8000 elsewhere – were being played not in the league that was suspended, but within a new regional competition format that cut the amount of travelling teams had to do. Ground managers had to employ raid spotters, who kept a look out for enemy aircraft and sounded a siren or some sort of recognised warning, if they spotted any while matches were in progress.

At first, the blackout kept many people at home in the evenings, but it was not long before the lure of the cinema outweighed the difficulties of getting there and home again through dark streets. Few cinemas closed, even during the worst days of the Blitz (unless completely destroyed, as some sixty London cinemas were during the war), although there were temporary closures for war damage repairs. Many cinema managers found that their dress circles were distinctly under-patronised, except by courting couples, during the Blitz. Going to the pictures became Britain's most popular away-from-home activity during the war. The country's approximately 5,000 cinemas, many of which had room for 2,500 seats, attracted millions of customers. By 1945, ticket sales had reached thirty million a week, despite regular increases in ticket prices.

◄ *Wartime Dance Hall*
A dance event for British and American service personnel at Covent Garden Opera House in London.

1943
MARCH

1 Battle of the Bismarck Sea north-east of New Guinea. Germans begin a withdrawal from Tunisia, Africa.

6 Germans attack Medenine, Tunisia.

15 Germans recapture Kharkov.

16 Battle of Atlantic reaches climax with 27 merchant ships sunk by German U-boats.

20 Montgomery's Eighth Army wins Battle of Mareth Line in Tunisia.

26 Battle of Komandorski Island.

APRIL

4 Allies bomb Naples, Syracuse and Sardinia.

6 Axis forces in Tunisia begin withdrawal towards Enfidaville as US and British forces link.

19 Warsaw Ghetto uprising, 60,000 Jews killed.

MAY

7 Allies take Tunisia.

13 German and Italian troops surrender in North Africa.

16 Jewish resistance in Warsaw Ghetto ends.
British air raid on the Ruhr.

22 Allies win Battle of Atlantic. Dönitz suspends U-boat operations in North Atlantic.

30 Bomb on Torquay church kills 290 children.

▲ *Moving Art*
September 1942: Attendants
take the painting 'Mother and
Child', of the Botticelli school,
out of storage for routine
inspection in a subterranean
chamber at Manod Quarry,
north Wales, where paintings
from the National Gallery
have been moved for safe
keeping during wartime.

DOING THE WARTIME POOLS

During the war, even in the darkest days of the Blitz and the V-1 and V-2 bombings, people could dream of winning the jackpot on the pools. The football pools continued throughout the war, offering betting on regional competition matches or on the 'War Cup' competition that replaced the FA Cup in March 1940. All football pools were pooled to form the 'Unity Pool', with the names of eight pre-war pools promoters, including Littlewoods and Vernons, at the top of the coupon. No less than one shilling (5p) could be invested on one coupon.

▲ *Mobile Film Screen*
October 1940: A crowd watches a film about the RAF on an outdoor screen aboard a mobile movie truck; the mobile screenings are used to raise money for weapons and general war effort during the days of the Battle of Britain, London, England.

1943

JUNE

1 Eden announces Empire casualties for first three years of war – 92,089 killed, 266,719 wounded.

2 Russians bomb Kiev and Rostov as Luftwaffe bombs Kursk.

10 'Point blank' directive to improve Allied bombing strategy issued.

11 Himmler orders the liquidation of all Jewish ghettos in Poland.
Allies invade Pantelleria.

18 Field Marshal Wavell appointed Viceroy of India.

19 Goebbels claims Berlin free of Jews.

20 RAF starts 'shuttle' bombing raids.

JULY

5 Germans begin their last offensive against Kursk.
Naval battle breaks out in Kula Gulf, north of New Georgia.

9 Allies land in Sicily.

19 Allies bomb Rome.

22 Americans capture Palermo, Sicily.

24 British bombing raid on Hamburg.

25 Mussolini arrested; Italian Fascist government falls.
Marshal Pietro Badoglio takes over and negotiates with Allies.

27 Allied air raid causes a firestorm in Hamburg.

29 Evacuation of a million civilians from Hamburg.
Third RAF raid on Hamburg.

Cinemas (and theatres) dealt with bombing raids by announcing during the performance that an air-raid warning had been received, leaving their patrons to decide for themselves if they would take shelter, perhaps in the building's basement, or continue watching the show, which was not stopped. As the war went on and a general shrug-of-the-shoulders fatalism set in, more and more people stayed in their seats.

British film-makers did not have the country's cinemas to themselves, for a large part of the output of Hollywood reached Britain during the war. One of the longest-running and most popular films in the country was *Gone With the Wind*, the film of Margaret Mitchell's great novel about the South during the American Civil War. Starring the British actors Vivien Leigh and Lesley Howard, as well as the wonderfully handsome and dashing Clark Gable, this Hollywood three-and-a-half-hour-long block-buster played to packed houses from its opening in London's Leicester Square in April 1940 until the end of its run in the summer of 1944.

Theatre life, especially in London, was rather different from that of the cinemas. When the Blitz was at its height, many theatres, attracting very small audiences and therefore disastrously low ticket sales, closed altogether, leaving only the Windmill, purveyor of nudity and comedy in London, to carry on.

◀ *Bombed Out Cinema*
1941: The ruins of a south London cinema, showing a poster that survived intact.

The worst of the Blitz over, theatre-going got into its stride again, with musicals, both British and American, being particularly popular, while comedies proved more popular than political or war-themed dramas, because they offered the greater escape from what was going on outside the theatre. The problems of the blackout made matinees particularly attractive choices for many, while evening performances in many theatres began as early as six o'clock – and with the pre-war evening dress convention for everyone in the stalls conspicuous by its absence.

Outside London, once theatres were permitted to open again, repertory theatres suffered for a time from an influx of London West End stars moving to the safety of the provinces and into touring productions, where their star quality drew audiences away from local theatre productions. On the whole, however, theatre outside London took on a new vigour during the war, taking advantage of the general recognition that cinema and the theatre could do much to boost morale in

1943
AUGUST

6 Battle of Vela Gulf, three Japanese ships sunk.
11 Germany begins night evacuation of Sicily.
13 Roosevelt and Churchill meet at the start of the Quebec Conference.
16 Heavy US air attacks on Japanese airfields on New Guinea.
17 US daylight air raids on Regensburg and Schweinfurt in Germany.
   Allies reach Messina, Sicily.
23 Soviet troops recapture Kharkov.
   RAF drop over 1,700 tons of bombs on Berlin.
25 Mountbatten appointed Supreme Allied Commander of SE Asia Command.
29 Martial law declared in Denmark.

BRITISH CINEMA'S GOLDEN AGE

Among the many fine films made in Britain during the war was many with a war theme. Films like Noel Coward's *In Which We Serve*, Powell and Pressburger's *49th Parallel* and *The Life and Death of Colonel Blimp*, Lauder and Gilliat's *Millions Like Us*, and – perhaps the finest and most patriotic of them all – Laurence Olivier's *Henry V*, remain classics of British film-making.

Even more popular, especially among women, were the wonderfully glamorous and melodramatic period concoctions of Gainsborough Studios, with their beautiful women, usually clad in low-cut, bosom-revealing gowns, and handsome, usually romantically wicked men.

wartime. Actors were able to claim exemption from military service, provided they were in more-or-less full-time work in the theatre or films (two consecutive weeks out of work, and military service loomed). Many stage and film actors managed to combine quite lengthy periods of military service with making films or acting in the theatre. Both Laurence Olivier and Ralph Richardson, for instance, spent some time in the Fleet Air Arm.

Despite the popularity of the cinema and, to a lesser extent, theatres, concert halls, dance halls and pubs, the home remained the place where the vast majority of people got most of their entertainment. While low-wattage light bulbs and wartime economy standard (i.e. poor quality) paper made reading at night difficult for some, curling up with a good book remained a particularly popular way of passing an evening at home

– or in the ARP post or anti-aircraft gun emplacement. Particularly popular wartime reading included the crime stories of Agatha Christie or Raymond Chandler and the classics of an earlier, quieter age of fiction-writing, such as the works of Charles Dickens and Anthony Trollope. The publishing of new books was drastically reduced during the war, with the 1945 total number of books published being less than half that of 1939.

For families at home together, radio provided the greatest entertainment. Well aware that it was responsible as much for keeping people's spirits up as for keeping them fully informed about the war's progress, the BBC provided hours and hours of dance music, variety shows and comedy shows on its Home Service. During the day, programmes aimed at specific audiences – householders with *The Kitchen Front* and *In Your Garden*,

ENSA

The Entertainments National Service Association (ENSA) was formed, at the instigation of the distinguished theatre director Basil Dean, to take entertainment to the services and those connected with them in Britain and overseas. Sometimes unfairly mocked for the quality of its shows

– there were people who said that 'ENSA' stood for 'Every Night Something Awful' – ENSA took its morale-boosting light entertainments all over Britain and overseas to the many places where British troops were fighting; ENSA's jokes were said to get bluer the nearer the troops were to the front line.

1943
SEPTEMBER

3 Allies start invasion of Italy.
7 Himmler and Göring order evacuation of Ukraine.
8 Italian surrender is announced.
9 Allied landings at Salerno and Taranto.
11 Germans occupy Rome.
12 Germans rescue Mussolini.
23 Mussolini re-establishes a Fascist government.
25 Soviets take Smolensk and Roslaul.
27 Allied air raids on Wewak, New Guinea, destroy 64 Japanese aircraft.
30 Danish Jews rounded up by Gestapo and Danish Nazis.

OCTOBER

1 Allies enter Naples, Italy.
4 Germans recapture island of Cos.
Himmler gives speech at Posen.
13 Italy declares war on Germany.
Second US air raid on Schweinfurt.
23 Russia takes Melitopol after ten days of fighting.
25 Japan opens infamous Burma-Sian railway built by forced POW labour.
26 Germany repatriates 790 wounded POWs to Britain.

children with *Children's Hour* (deemed too flippant for wartime in September 1939 and cancelled, but hastily re-instated), factory workers with *Workers' Playtime* and *Music While You Work* – filled the airwaves.

In February 1940, the BBC launched the *General Forces Programme*, aimed specifically at the men and women of the armed forces, and including programmes like *Forces Favourites, Calling the Forces Everywhere* and *Navy Mixture*. Vera Lynn, the 'Forces' Sweetheart' and the most popular singer of the war, became famous through her appearances on the *Forces Programme*. When the BBC began rebuilding its radio network in the summer of 1945, the *Forces Programme* was renamed the *Light Programme*. It and the *Home Service* were joined by the *Third Programme* in 1946, the year when television began broadcasting again. (Shut down completely in 1939, British television did not really begin to establish itself as a mass medium until the Coronation of Elizabeth II in 1953.)

◀ *ENSA At Drury Lane*
An ENSA (Entertainment National Services Association) touring group preparing for a tour at the ENSA headquarters in Drury Lane, London.

1943
NOVEMBER

6   Russians recapture Kiev.

18   Large British air raid on Berlin.

22   Cairo Conference – Roosevelt, Churchilll and Chiang Kai-shek.

28   Roosevelt, Churchill and Stalin meet at Teheran Summit Conference.

DECEMBER

2   Conscription for active service introduced for Hitler youth.

11   Heavy US air raid on Emden kills 1,000.

18   German war criminals sentenced to death at Kharkov war crimes trial.

24   Soviets launch offensives on Ukraine.

At night, the family would gather round the wireless in the living room to enjoy together such comedy programmes as ITMA (*It's That Man Again*), starring Tommy Handley, Kenneth Horne's *Much Binding In the Marsh*, and the rather more intellectually challenging *Brain's Trust*. And there were hours of ballroom dance music, led by such famous band leaders as Henry Hall, Geraldo, Victor Sylvester and, later in the war, the American Glen Miller, and often broadcast direct from such glamorous places as the Savoy Ballroom.

It was while sitting round the wireless in the living room that most people first heard of the great events that were happening in their country and in the rest of the world. Neville Chamberlain announced that the country was at war with Germany on the radio and Winston Churchill, his famously rumbling deep voice already familiar to his listeners, announced the end of the war in 1945 on the *BBC Home Service*, before he officially informed the House of Commons.

The war made radio performers and newsreaders – no less than comedy stars and band leaders – the celebrities of the age. The BBC placed great emphasis on the names as well as the voices of their newsreaders being familiar – 'This is the news and this is Alvar Lidell reading it' – because it lessened the likelihood of German broadcasting of morale-damaging propaganda being believed.

The notorious Irish-born William Joyce (called 'Lord Haw Haw' because of his upper-class accent), who broadcast pro-German propaganda from Hamburg and regularly picked up an audience of millions during the Phoney War, lost most of his audience when the war got serious. The BBC lessened the chances of German imposters being able to copy English accents successfully by using many more people like the northerner Wilfrid Pickles who spoke with regional accents rather than with the 'Received Pronunciation' that had been de rigeur for newsreaders (along with wearing dinner jackets to read the evening news) in the 1930s.

Thus the BBC, a bastion of pre-war middle-class values, made a major contribution to the social revolution that World War II brought about in Britain.

▶ *Listening In*
2 August 1941: The clientele of a London pub listen to the radio during the broadcast of one of Churchill's speeches.

LISTENING TO THE WIRELESS

Nine million wireless receiving licences were issued in Britain in 1939 – enough to ensure that some ninety per cent of households had a wireless. Manufacturers responded to wartime demand by producing both wirelesses and radiograms with increased short-wave facilities and better tuning systems. There were more battery-operated models, too. Thus, even if you were sitting in your blackout-dim house or holed up in your Anderson shelter, you could listen to the wireless.

VICTORY AND AFTER

The Allies took the war against Germany into Europe, first from North Africa into Italy and Greece, and then, in June 1944 in the great D-Day landings, from the south of England, which for months had been virtually an armed camp. In the Far East, the war against Japan also moved into a new, even more aggressive phase in 1944, with the Philippines being re-captured by the Americans in October, and Japan's mainland being bombed in November.

But the war was not yet over for Britain, either on the mainland or in the Channel Islands. Even as the Allies, advancing across northern Europe, were crossing the Rhine, Hitler unleashed his V-1 and V-2 weapons against England. It was not until 7 May 1945 that Germany, Hitler having committed suicide in his Berlin bunker, surrendered. The next day, VE Day – Victory in Europe Day – saw cheering and flag-waving crowds throughout Britain – but not in the Channel Islands, which had to wait one more day to be relieved of the German occupation, which had become increasingly harsh.

On 8 May 1945, Winston Churchill, standing on the balcony of the Ministry of Health in London, led the cheering crowd celebrating victory in Europe in a rousing rendition of 'Land of Hope and Glory'. Little did he and the government figures around him think that less than three months later he would be rejected as the nation's leader in Britain's first peacetime general election, in which the Labour Party, led by Clement Attlee, was swept into power.

So it was Clement Attlee, not Winston Churchill, who announced the absolute end of World War II in August 1945. By the time of VJ Day – Victory over Japan Day – the world had discovered the full, dreadful horror of the Nazi death camps, and British soldiers had burnt one of them, Burgen-Belsen, to the ground in May.

Probably many who had been in that exuberantly joyful crowd outside the Ministry of Health in May were not very surprised by Labour's victory. The way in which the war had been fought by what J. B. Priestley, in one of his hugely popular Postscripts radio broadcasts, had called 'the organised militant citizen', had brought about a major revolution in social attitudes and expectations in Britain. Twenty-five million people, including some 1,700,000 servicemen and women, voted in the 1945 General Election, with three votes out of every five being cast against the Conservatives. No one wanted to return to the unemployment, poverty for many and class-dividing social policies of the 1930s.

Britain's working classes had become better off during the war. There had been full employment and good wages, both made possible by the dynamic interventionist policies pursued by the government. At the same time, the appalling conditions under which too many working-class people lived, revealed by such things as the poor

▲ *Start Of VE Day*
19 May 1945: The cover of a Victory Special issue of Picture Post *magazine, depicting a mother and her two sons celebrating VE Day in Britain, at the end of World War II.*

condition of many of the children evacuated from inner cities to the middle-class suburbs and country towns and villages, emphasised the need for a properly organised and funded welfare system.

Long before the war was over there had been much discussion about the shape that post-war British society should take. In 1941, the Board of Education had begun planning for a new education system, and a committee, chaired by a leading civil servant, William

1944
JANUARY

1 Soviet troops advance into Poland.
4 Germans announce school-children to be used for war work.
14 Russians launch new offensive around Leningrad.
17 First attack towards Cassino, Italy.
22 Allies land at Anzio.
26 British launch main attack on Japanese 'Golden Fortress' in the Arakan, Burma.
27 Leningrad relieved after a 900-day siege.
29 Luftwafe penetrates London.
800 USAAF bombers hit Frankfurt.
31 Land fighting begins in Dutch New Guinea.

FEBRUARY

1 Polish underground execute chief of Gestapo in Poland.
15 Allies bomb the monastery at Monte Cassino.
16 Germans counter-attack against Anzio beachhead.

MARCH

4 Soviet troops begin an offensive on the Belrussian Front.
15 Second Allied attempt to capture Monte Cassino.
18 British drop 3,000 tons of bombs during an air raid on Hamburg.
24 Battle of Berlin over.

▶ *Returning Soldiers*
1945: Soldiers returning from Europe after D-Day, on a London Underground train.

▲ *Cause for celebration*
7 May 1945: Men atop a lightpost during unofficial eve of VE Day celebration, marking the end of World War II in Europe.

Idleness – that kept too many people in poverty. The Report was the foundation on which the 1945 Labour government built Britain's new welfare state.

The new Labour government found itself dealing with enormous social problems in a country that many thought would never be prosperous again, so great had been the cost of fighting and winning the war. It was vital that there should be no repeat of the post-Great War failure to make Britain a land 'fit for heroes'. All returning servicemen must have jobs to go to, there must be homes for them and their families to live in, and schools to give their children a proper education.

Returning servicemen and women, brought home in manageable numbers over many months and given the de-mob suit or clothing to which they were entitled when returning to Civvy Street, found jobs more quickly than their fathers had after 1918. The government, still very much in dynamic directive mode, directed the return to work by dividing workers into two classes, A and B. The B workers – those who had had trades and crafts before the war that could be used again – were given jobs, using the skills they already had: once a plumber, always a plumber in immediate post-war Britain.

For those not in the B group, finding a job was not so easy. Many firms had disappeared altogether and most others needed time to get back into full peacetime production. Even so, the government could feel some satisfaction in the knowledge that by the end of 1945 some 750,000 servicemen and

Beveridge, was set up to make a comprehensive study of existing health insurance and other social security schemes and to suggest better ways of providing these. The main concern of the Beveridge Report, which was published in December 1943, was to emphasise the necessity of creating a comprehensive policy of social progress and social security in Britain, in order to overcome the five giants – Want, Disease, Ignorance, Squalor and

THE BEVERIDGE REPORT

The Beveridge Report proposed nothing less than a revolution, involving cooperation between the state and the individual, in the way social security was provided in Britain. The welfare state that could be said to have been born in Britain on 5 July 1948, the day when the new National Insurance Scheme and the National Health Service came into operation, developed directly out of the Beveridge Report.

1944
APRIL

8 Soviet troops begin an offensive to liberate Crimea.
10 RAF drop a record 3,600 tons of bombs over Northern France.
12 Hitler authorises Crimean withdrawals.
13 British retake Nunshigum Hill, Burma.
Simferopol, Feodosiya and Eupatoria fall to Red Army.
14 Russian troops take Tarnopol.

MAY

9 Russians capture Sevastopol.
11 Allies attack the Gustav Line south of Rome.
12 Germans surrender in Crimea.
15 Germans withdraw to the Adolf Hitler Line.
18 British capture Cassino monastery.
23 Allies launch massive breakout at Anzio.
25 Germans retreat from Anzio.

JUNE

5 Allies enter Rome.
6 D-Day landings.
7 Allies liberate Bayeux.
9 Soviet offensive against the Finnish front begins.
13 First German V-1 rocket attack on Britain.
19 Two-day Battle of the Philippine Sea starts.
22 Operation Bagration begins.
27 US troops liberate Cherbourg.

1944

JULY

3 Battle of the Hedgerows in Normandy.
Soviets capture Minsk.
25 Operation Cobra – US breakout from Normandy.
28 Soviet troops take Brest-Litovsk.

AUGUST

1 US troops reach Avranches.
15 Operation Dragoon begins, the Allied invasion of Southern France.
20 Russians attack Romania.
25 Liberation of Paris.
30 Germans start pulling out of Bulgaria.
31 Soviet troops take Bucharest.

SEPTEMBER

4 Finland and Soviet Union agree to a ceasefire.
13 US troops reach the Siegfried Line.

OCTOBER

2 Warsaw Uprising ends.

NOVEMBER

8 USAAF start 72-day bombing of Iwo Jima.

DECEMBER

4 Civil War in Greece; Athens placed under martial law.
16 Battle of the Bulge in the Ardennes.
26 Patton relieves Bastogne.
27 Soviet troops besiege Budapest.

women were back in jobs on Civvy Street. There were also many resettlement and training schemes, aimed at providing the extra 800,000 properly trained people the government estimated they would need to get the post-war economy on the move.

One particularly effective training scheme grew out of the wartime recognition that providing Britain's children with a good education was clearly an essential element of welfare state planning: if Ignorance was not defeated, then the giant Idleness, created by unemployment and causing poverty, could not be defeated either. The intensive training scheme for teachers enabled candidates, many of whom did their study while still on army bases, to obtain a teaching diploma in one year. Britain's schools, whose part in the education of the nation had been dramatically changed and enhanced by the 1944 Education Act, gained some 45,000 men and women teachers through the scheme.

The design of one of the special postage stamps issued to mark VE Day incorporated a dove of peace, a trowel, set square and dividers – an acknowledgement, if any were needed, that reconstruction was going to be the major problem facing the new government. As with social welfare and education, the government had recognised long before the war was over that rebuilding Britain was going to be a very big post-victory task. In 1943, Lord Woolton was moved from the Ministry of Food to head a new Ministry of Reconstruction.

It wasn't just a question of rebuilding the properties destroyed in the war and refurbishing those that had been

THE BUTLER EDUCATION ACT

The Education Act of 1944, usually called the Butler Education Act, after R. A. Butler, President of the Board of Education, raised the school-leaving age to 15 and provided free secondary education for all children, following selection at 11. The Act also incorporated other benefits established as part of the developing family welfare system, such as free milk for children and a subsidised school meals service for all children, regardless of their parents' income.

▲ *Prefab Estate*
April 1946: Schoolchildren helping the workmen construct a new estate of prefabricated houses in Watford, Hertfordshire, after the devastation of World War II.

damaged but were still habitable. It was obvious by September 1944, when official figures were published showing that 200,000 houses had been destroyed in Britain and another 4 million damaged, that it was not going to be simply a matter of replacing them. There had been two million marriages in Britain since the start of the war, and the birth rate was rising. Many more houses would have to be built after the war than had been built in an average year before it.

The government aimed to have the majority of house rebuilding carried out by local authorities. It passed a Housing Act in 1946 that guaranteed subsidies and grants for new housing, setting a target of 240,000 new homes a year. But both manpower and building materials were in very short supply in the immediate post-war years and Labour's target proved unreachable. Various alternative housing stop-gaps were employed, including temporary homes and prefabricating housing. It was not until the Conservatives were back in power – the Labour party losing the 1952 general election largely because they had failed to provide enough new housing – that housing targets were reached.

As for that other great wartime horror – rationing – everyone's hopes that the new government would end it as soon as possible, were quickly dashed. The post-war government had huge bills to pay, not least the one to the United States for the vast wartime Lend-Lease programme. It would be some years before people could throw away their ration books and their coupons – some, such as petrol coupons, having been valuable enough to replace sixpenny bits in the wartime Christmas pudding (a surprisingly delicious variation on Lord Woolton's pie, based on carrots, spices and the brown and unlovely National Flour).

Food rationing, which had, in fact, provided many of Britain's poorer people with the first really adequate diet they had ever known, lasted the longest. Butter, margarine and fat rations had to be cut in early 1946. Within months, bread, which had remained unrationed throughout the war, was also rationed, followed by potatoes (also unrationed during the war) in November 1947. These rationings were caused partly by a world-wide food shortage and partly by poor harvests that followed a very cold winter in 1946–47. The stopping of the United State's Lend-Lease programme, two days after VJ Day in August 1945, had not helped the food situation, either, with American dried-egg powder among the ingredients suddenly no longer available.

By 1950, most of the country's food shortages had been relieved – helped by a splendid 'Bonfire of Controls' carried out by Harold Wilson, President of the Board of Trade, in November 1948. Individual foods began gradually to be taken off the ration. To the delight of children and their parents alike, sweet rationing was abolished in February

▲ *Bread Queues*
20 July 1946: Queues forming outside a bakery in Streatham High Street, London, on the last day before bread rationing is introduced.

PREFABRICATED MODERNITY

Building houses in the same way that aircraft had been turned out during the war seemed an obvious solution to Britain's post-war housing problems. By 1944, prefabricated houses were being made, quickly and cheaply, on the assembly lines of factories that had once turned out aircraft and armaments. The first prefabs – as these houses were soon known – were put up in London in April 1944. Built in three days, they cost £550 each. There were various styles, including a flat-roofed 'box bungalow' with a living room, a built-in kitchen recess, two bedrooms and a bathroom, and a semi-tubular Nissen hut-shaped house. Prefabs were intended to last only ten years. Many of them were still in use – and much loved by their occupants – several decades later.

1945
JANUARY

1/ Germans withdraw from
17 the Ardennes.

FEBRUARY

4 Yalta Conference between Churchill, Roosevelt and Stalin opens.
7 Germans blow up floodgates on Ruhr.
13 Dresden destroyed after Allied bombing raids.

MARCH

30 Soviet troops capture Danzig.

APRIL

1 US troops encircle Germans in Ruhr.
18 German forces in the Ruhr surrender.
28 Mussolini is captured and hanged by Italian parisans. Allies take Venice.
30 Adolf Hitler commits suicide.

MAY

2 German troops in Italy surrender.
7 Unconditional surrender of all German forces to Allies.
8 VE Day (Victory for Europe).
9 Hermann Göring is captured by members of the US 7th Army.
23 SS Reichsführer Himmler commits suicide.
German High Command and Provisional Government imprisoned.

▲ VE Ride
8 May 1945: VE Day revellers on a lorry in London.

1953 and the last two rationed foods, butter and meat, were taken off rations in 1954.

Furniture rationing ended in the summer of 1948 and Utility furniture, with its attractive exemption from Purchase Tax, was phased out in 1953. Clothes rationing was abolished in 1949 (at much the same time as the milk ration had to be cut to two pints a week).

The awful wartime austerity, which had gone on for so long, seemed at last to be over and Britain, with a young and lovely queen recently crowned in the first really splendidly ceremonial occasion anyone had seen for many years, began to think it really could look forward to a New Elizabethan Age.

▲ *Buying Sweets*
April 1953: Customers, including some eager schoolboys, buying sweets in a sweet shop now that they are no longer rationed.